"Dr Poole's work is a magnificent contribution to th
Written by a gifted theologian and pract
all those wishing to gain both a richer th(
of capitalism and modern consumerism, a
on how we can simplify our lives. This is v
our own spiritual benefit, but also for the g
for the wellbeing of our planet." *The Most .
Honourable Justin Welby, Archbishop of Ca*

"This is a wonderful book. It is very accessible, theologically
sophisticated, and rooted in a deep knowledge of commerce,
management and consumerism, in which Eve Poole is an expert.
I know of no better book for guiding Christians in the day to day
world of consumerism. Inspiring, compelling and very easy to
read, it deserves a wide readership." *Peter Sedgwick, theologian
and former Principal of St. Michael's College, Llandaff*

"This learned and thought provoking book might be the only
you ever need on the subject. It manages to combine a whistle
stop tour through theology's big dogs with a helpful primer
on capitalism and some deeply practical questions to provoke
action. It's rare that a book this readable and amusing covers so
much intellectual ground." *Elizabeth Oldfield, Director, Theos*

"Knowledgeable and accessible, as adept at exploring economics
as at delineating theological method, *Buying God* offers a steady
hand through the demands of global capitalism and the seductions
of human desire. Eve Poole offers an example of how theology is
always politics, and always devotional – and, at its best, both at the
same time." *Samuel Wells, Vicar of St Martin-in-the-Fields*

"This book is thought provoking, giving the reader the opportunity to reflect seriously from a theological perspective about their
own consumerism and the wider implications of consumerism
within the global economy." *Revd Dr Fiona Stewart-Darling,
Bishop's Chaplain in London Docklands*

Buying God

Consumerism and Theology

Eve Poole

scm press

© Eve Poole 2018

Published in 2018 by SCM Press
Editorial office
3rd Floor, Invicta House,
108–114 Golden Lane,
London EC1Y 0TG, UK
www.scmpress.co.uk

SCM Press is an imprint of Hymns Ancient & Modern Ltd
(a registered charity)

Hymns Ancient & Modern® is a registered trademark of Hymns
Ancient & Modern Ltd
13A Hellesdon Park Road, Norwich,
Norfolk NR6 5DR, UK

Scripture quotations are from the New Revised Standard Version
of the Bible, Anglicized Edition, copyright © 1989, 1995 by the
Division of Christian Education of the National Council of the
Churches of Christ in the USA. Used by permission.
All rights reserved.

British Library Cataloguing in Publication data

A catalogue record for this book is available
from the British Library

978 0 334 05674 4

Typeset by Manila Typesetting Company
Printed and bound by CPI Group (UK) Ltd

Contents

And so the yearning strong, with which the soul
will long,
Shall far outpass the power of human telling;
For none can guess its grace, till he become the place
Wherein the Holy Spirit makes His dwelling.

Bianco da Siena, trans. Richard Frederick Littledal

Preface

This book was commissioned to bring together into one volume my work to date on theology, capitalism and consumerism. Much of this is buried in monographs, scattered between blogs and sermons, or contained in several seemingly unconnected books. Some of the content may therefore not be new to those who have followed my work, but the opportunity this volume provides is to draw the threads together into a coherent argument. It seeks to make sense of my disparate thoughts, and to contribute towards the wider debate on how we as Christians should behave in the marketplace, both individually and collectively.

As will be argued in the book, the person of the theologian is particularly pertinent in the matter of public theology. Therefore, some context follows. I was brought up a cradle Christian in the Scottish Episcopal Church. I read Theology at Durham before working for the Church Commissioners for England as a graduate. I then took an MBA at Edinburgh and worked for Deloitte Consulting as a Change Management Consultant in London, with a particular focus on the financial services sector. I left this profession to teach leadership at Ashridge Business School, and to study part-time at Cambridge for a PhD in Capitalism and Theology. I became freelance when I had children, and now occupy non-executive roles as the Chairman of Gordonstoun and as the Third Church Estates Commissioner. I have written several books on marketplace theology and leadership, all of which are independent of any of my employers. I write as a Christian who is a member of the Church of England but who has worked enough in a secular context to appreciate that neither has a monopoly on the truth. My style is deliberately accessible and will not appeal to those who prefer a higher academic tone. Neither do I locate myself within any specific church tradition. My intention is to inform and to persuade, and I own a bias towards practical action rather than just the right thoughts.

Thanks are due to Palgrave Macmillan, Bloomsbury and the William Temple Foundation for permission to include some material from my earlier publications. The analysis of type first appeared in a thesis I submitted for my PhD. It was subsequently published as *The Church on Capitalism* (Poole 2010). Material from Chapter 3 of that book is reproduced here with kind permission of Palgrave Macmillan. Detailed academic footnotes appear in that volume but are omitted in this one. A shorter version of that analysis also appeared in *Theology and Economics* (Kidwell and Doherty 2015). A version of the argument about Capitalism was first delivered as the Just Share Lecture at St Mary-le-Bow on 29 January 2014. The full argument appears in *Capitalism's Toxic Assumptions* (Poole 2015a). I also wrote two ebooks for the William Temple Foundation, *God and Money* (Poole 2015b) and *Ethical Consumerism* (Poole 2016), elements of which are reproduced here; and a fuller discussion of character and habits in the context of leadership can be found in *Leadersmithing* (Poole 2017).

I am particularly grateful to Nathan Percival, Peter Sedgwick, Ann Loades and Philip Krinks for their encouragement and support. You have to be either arrogant or brave to be a theologian, because you risk heresy with everything you write. So I am in debt to all the wise souls who have tried to keep me on the straight path – any resulting heresy is of course all mine.

Introduction

Why did you buy this book? Its title is *Buying God*. Did you think that was what you were doing? Of course it is a play on words. We need to buy God not Mammon in our purchasing; but also, if we are ever to rescue our economic system from collapse, consumerism needs to buy God as providing a better explanatory narrative than Mammon. Addiction to growth, novelty and accumulation is putting us on a collision course with the planet. We shall not win, because the planet will just kick us off if we go too far. That means that we need to correct our consumerism, and to find ways to live together, sustainably.

The book starts with an extended section on theological method. It uses the fruits of this analysis to shape the second half, which is a practical look at consumerism in context; what theology might have to say about it; and a concluding section about how we as Christians might sow the seeds of the transformation of consumerism.

You are the consumer, so you can read it however you like. Here are some suggestions:

- If you tend to read books from cover to cover, thank you and congratulations – you are a rare beast.
- If you are in the trade, you might like the theology section, although it will make you wince a bit.
- If you are feeling anxious about consumerism, you might like to focus on the consumer audit at the end.

- If you are a student, I've tried to make the referencing light but obvious – please get in touch if you need more.
- If you are writing a sermon for the weekend, use the Index to find the quirky bits.
- If you are involved in Christian formation, use the Resources section to help you cure your souls.

This preamble shows that my primary audience for this book is my fellow believers. I hope it will help all of us to feel braver about accounting for the hope that is in us, because the world needs to hear what we have to say. In an often openly hostile context, finding our voice in the public square is difficult, and this book should help to arm us for that fight. And it is a fight. The unquestioning acceptance of secularism as a 'neutral' narrative has allowed consumerism free rein. But we can see that all is not well, because the have-nots in our parishes the length and breadth of the country are not profiting from the 'trickle down' that capitalism promised. As I will argue, our sort of Christianity is uniquely perfect for the task in hand. So we need to put on the armour of Christ and get to work. And if any of you are reading this as a non-Christian out of curiosity? Welcome. We need you too.

Theory of Change

Because this is so important, I do not want to miss out any steps, even if you choose to do so. Ignore me if so. But it has become fashionable to discuss 'theories of change' when embarking upon any project that is exhortative in nature. And because the intent of this book is to inspire consumer action, it is right to own the assumptions being made about what needs to change and how change happens.

In the first instance, I want to talk about systems, through the device of the Orders of Creation. Then I want to bridge into people versus systems, through the work of Douglas Griffin. Finally,

I want to look at salt and light through the lens of the game theorists.

Orders of Creation

There is a rather neglected motif in theology known as Orders of Creation. The term, more familiar to continental audiences than within Anglican theology, seeks to address the very practical problem facing adults that, by the time they are in a position to notice their formation and to develop opinions about it, most of it has already happened. This means that there is never an untainted vantage point, where influences such as family and society have not already made their mark. This renders it hazardous to affect the objective nonchalance of scholarship without at least exploring what some of those formative influences have already been, and how they might already be refracting the argument.

Bonhoeffer called them the Mandates, Barth the Provinces; but most sources agree that the Orders are marriage and the family, the economic order, the political order and the community of culture. Ronald Preston, who often discusses them in his work, explains that these Orders affect humans before they are able to notice or make choices, and their decisive influence demands that in any debate involving them, what is required is the concurrent reformation of both the structures themselves and the individuals influenced by them: to focus on either to the detriment of the other prevents progress (Preston 1979, pp. 76f.).

Discussion about the Orders points up the chicken-and-egg matter of the extent to which structures influence individuals and are influenced by them. Views on how best to resolve this dilemma produce a spectrum among commentators from an emphasis on concrete changes to policy, systems or institutions, on the one hand, to an emphasis on the necessary reform of individuals – both in heart, mind and behaviour – on the other.

Institutions

Consumerism is clearly part of the economic order, so we cannot look at it dispassionately, having already been formed by it. So how can we achieve a critical distance? Douglas Griffin is our first port of call. He notes our tendency to blame 'the system' when things go wrong, even while we have been autonomous moral actors within it. This is, simply, duplicitous (Griffin 2002, pp. 1ff.). Of course we are shaped by Orders of Creation – or any system – but we can also shape them in turn: both/and, not either/or. Wherever we see organizations being called out for bad behaviour, it would have been entirely possible for their members to have spontaneously reformed if they had felt strongly enough about it.

This rather tough line is given credence by the work of Douglass North, located within the wider literature on institutions. His work on institutions has been developed by Anthony Kasozi into a useful taxonomy. After North, Kasozi defines institutions as 'socially established rules, or systems of rules, that systematically organize, enable and constrain all human beings and interactions in a society' (Kasozi 2008, p. 112). He draws a distinction between institutions and mere influences, and describes four families of institutions:

1 Language, which underpins and provides the foundation for all other institutions.
2 Explicit Institutions, which are public rules and systems of rules, like constitutions, laws and legal systems, decrees, money, conventions, codes, contracts and property rights.
3 Implicit Institutions, which are those unwritten rules that are held commonly within a given social grouping, like a norm or a custom, some of which underpin many of the categories above.
4 Other 'Complex' Institutions, which vary in appearance and intricacy depending on the nature and complexity of the civil society in which they develop, like family, clan, organization, market, state (Kasozi 2008, pp. 115f., Table 3.1, pp. 120f.).

His categories are not mutually exclusive, so a given institution may resonate across the categories, but his classification opens up a far wider-ranging field than the traditional list of Orders, which it can also accommodate.

Whether the language used is one of Orders or institutions, one thing becomes abundantly clear: they are all man-made, and so can be un-made. Sometimes such changes may seem like tasks for a Goliath; equally throughout history and all over the world such things have often been overturned by a David. And the Church is currently a Power in its own right. Episcopally led, and synodically governed. It would be entirely possible for the Church to engage with partner institutions – other Principalities and Powers – particularly where these intersect with the Church's wider mission and activities. Such an investigation would include a discussion of systems and complexity thinking, as well as the practices of dialogue and change, to ascertain how the Church might best understand, co-exist with, and influence modern institutions and culture. We will discuss a good example of this later on, when we look at the Church's recent initiative on consumer lending.

Salt and Light

We can influence institutions, and we can change our own behaviour. But does being salt and light really work? Game theory would suggest that it does. Game theory is a branch of mathematics that seeks to model interactions between intelligent and rational decision-makers, and is used in economics, politics and psychology, as well as in logic and programming. It reduces typical interactions to formulaic 'games' to test strategies and to predict likely outcomes. One such game is called the Prisoner's Dilemma. This basic scenario involves two suspects being arrested and imprisoned by the police. Because the evidence is insufficient for a conviction, the authorities need at least one of the suspects to confess in order that both might be implicated.

The prisoners are placed in separate cells, and the police visit each in turn to persuade them to confess. Obviously, if both prisoners remain silent, both will go free. If both confess, both will be sentenced. If one confesses, he could negotiate a reduced sentence in return for his cooperation. Given that the prisoners have no way to communicate, they have to guess how the other will act, and respond accordingly. Simple scenarios like this one are used by the game theorists to spot patterns and rules about how we interact with others, and can be applied in a wide variety of settings. For example, the Prisoner's Dilemma is the basic 'game' behind the arms race, and many trade and treaty negotiations, and any situation where cooperating or defecting are the basic choices available. In its simplest form, the Prisoner's Dilemma is what is called a 'zero sum' game, in that if one wins, the other loses. These 'games' can be modelled as one-off interactions, or can be iterated over time to see how strategies change in the light of past behaviour and experience.

As part of his exploration into the evolution of cooperation, Robert Axelrod describes a massive tournament of computerized games, submitted by a wide range of experts from diverse disciplines, all designed to play this classic game iteratively with one another. The tournament showed that by the one-thousandth generation the cooperative game called Tit for Tat (be nice, punish a defection once, resume being nice) was the most successful, and was growing at a faster rate than any other. He finds that in a system of 'games' that includes a mixture of 'nice' and 'mean' ones, the nice games will prevail. This is because the mean games destroy the environment they need for their own success, while the nice games 'train' the environment such that everybody benefits, ratcheting up their individual efforts and acting as a defence against subsequent 'invasion' by mean strategies. What is particularly attractive about this finding is that it suggests that individual and repeated actions in the marketplace can have exponentially positive effects, particularly where there are small clusters of players committed to deploying a nice strategy. Axelrod's analysis suggests that these effects are surprisingly simply won, because they are essentially self-organizing:

What is most interesting is how little had to be assumed about the individuals or the social setting to establish these results. The individuals do not have to be rational: the evolutionary process allows the successful strategies to thrive, even if the players do not know why or how. Nor do the players need to exchange messages or commitments: they do not need words, because their deeds speak for them. Likewise, there is no need to assume trust between the players: the use of reciprocity can be enough to make defection unproductive. Altruism is not needed: successful strategies can elicit cooperation even from an egoist. Finally, no central authority is needed: cooperation based on reciprocity can be self-policing. (Axelrod 1990, p. 173)

Leadership

So change is about both systems and people, and even small actions by those people can have an effect on the system over time. But no change will be compelling if those leading it are uncommitted and inconsistent. And those leading change will find it easier to maintain momentum if they are clear-eyed about the cost of change. Working for Deloitte as a change management consultant, I met a whole range of change models: houses, steps, grids, circles, transitions, pathways – as many models as there are gurus and consulting firms to sell them. I have not yet met one that was not based on the Kübler-Ross grief curve. It was devised by the Swiss psychiatrist Elisabeth Kübler-Ross in 1969, inspired by her work with the terminally ill, through research on death and those faced with it at the University of Chicago medical school. Her model is about the range of emotions typically experienced on the death of a loved one. The five stages are expressed as denial, anger, bargaining, depression and acceptance, and are often drawn as a u-shaped curve. She later extended her work to include any form of personal loss, such as job loss, loss of freedom, relationship break-up, or major illness.

Although the theological concept of metanoia is similar (μετάνοια), because it is first and foremost a turning away from something, to begin with I was rather suspicious about the connection between grief and change. Then I started using an exercise about change that asks people to pair up, change three things about their appearance, and see if their partner can spot them. Every single time I have run this exercise, every single person starts by losing something – a ring, a watch, a tie, a shoe – their instinct is to take something off. It is only after a few iterations of this exercise that people start adding things and borrowing things; copying, sharing and experimenting; all the kinds of positive behaviours that you really want during times of change. It seems inevitable that initial change will attract this instinctive response. So leaders need to hold their nerve and persist, if the change is going to have any lasting and positive effect.

This process of initially rejecting, then wrestling with, then integrating, new data, is how we learn anything new. But change is also about inertia. The human brain strives for efficiency, storing habits as heuristics to speed up cognitive processing. To re-write these programmes requires energy and effort, so an efficient system will only pay that price if it has to. In the change management literature this is referred to as the 'burning bridge', to communicate something of the imperative there needs to be for change to happen. From theology – rather than just Freudian psychology – we know that humans can and do choose alternative futures that will 'cost' them, not because they have to but because they want to. While these may attract future extrinsic rewards, they may also be motivated intrinsically, by moral goods to do with honour, the old-fashioned virtues and character-building.

In a commercial environment the prevailing utilitarian ethic assumes carrot-and-stick thinking, so volitional and altruistic positive action feels alien and can appear suspicious to others. It remains true that it feels easier to design a change process defended by a business case than it is to trust in human nature and the call of the divine, but as Christians we should not let ourselves be hoodwinked into thinking this is either normal or ideal. So the canny Christian leader of change might be wise as a serpent about who stands to win or lose, but also be gentle as a dove about what God is gracefully calling us to do, even when the prospect is unclear.

And now, to theology.

PART ONE

How to do Theology

I

Types of Theology

Introduction

If you are a theology nerd like me, you'll like this bit. If you would rather see the sum and not the working, please feel free to skip to the end. But beware: in doing so you will miss learning about what sort of God you really believe in, and why theologians should be more moody. And I have provided cheat sheets.

All theologians are up to something. Invariably they sound erudite and sure. They are part of a venerable tradition, in which the views of wise men tend to command respect. Before examining any given theology, though, it is helpful to understand what it is trying to do, and this is not always clear, given the particularly obfuscatory jargon the Church has always used both to convey its essential mystery and to signal intellectual superiority.

This section exists to contextualize my own contribution, so that it might be audited for theological health. It carries a jargon warning at the threat level of mild but prolonged, with some strong language. It is necessary, however, for producing two key results. The first is to establish the criteria that should be involved in testing any theology of capitalism (the hardware) or consumerism (the software). This is a healthcheck, so that when plausible and earnest theologians take to the marketplace, we can assess the strengths and weaknesses of their approach before swallowing it whole. I include myself in their number. The second is a happy accident, a by-product of the technical analysis of type, which reveals a hitherto under-served focus of theology.

The Theos term 'social liturgy' describes it (see p. 60). Because much of the rest of the book will be concerned with exploring how both the Church collectively and Christians individually might live out their beliefs in a consumerist world, this area of activity is particularly pertinent.

Normally in discussions of this kind, Middle Axioms appear first on the jargon bingo card. In Anglican Social Theology, and in the tradition of Archbishop William Temple, it is customary to preface any discussion of theology about matters of wider public interest with a discussion of middle axioms. This done, the argument proceeds as if nothing had happened, having ticked a theological box. This book will be a departure from that tradition, because it lays out a far wider theological context first. But because some readers may not be able to settle until they have seen middle axioms arrive on stage, here is a preliminary note about them.

The theologian Ronald Preston is most famously associated with middle axioms. The term was coined by J. H. Oldham, but Preston credits William Temple as the author of the process it describes. Preston championed the process in his writings and through his engagement with the Church of England's Board for Social Responsibility. He describes a middle axiom as 'half-way between a general principle and a detailed policy. It derives both from a general insight drawn from Christian faith, and from an empirical diagnosis of the present trends with respect to work, leading to a recommendation as to the direction in which it is desirable for social policy to go' (Preston 1987, pp. 130f.). The middle axiom approach is a particular feature of much Anglican Social Theology (see Brown 2014). Preston and his supporters argue that it should be the standard method for conducting Christian social ethics, comprising empirical analysis, theological commentary and directional principles, the latter being deliberately vague so as to be most useful to a broad church that also values moral autonomy. Of course, by design such an approach assumes an empirical epistemology, which tends to eclipse a more ontological theological approach, giving the discourse an innate methodological bias, which is rarely discussed. So while the feather bed of middle axioms looms large for any discussion of such an empirically manifest phenomenon as consumerism, this book will first do the heavy lifting on theology and theological method before proceeding towards conclusions.

Typing

I wonder what the collective noun would be for a room full of academics talking about theological method. A bore of theologians? As Jeffrey Stout says: 'preoccupation with method is like clearing your throat: it can go on only so long before you lose your audience' (Stout 1990, p. 163). But in talking about consumerism, market economics, or any topic that is claimed by the secular world, such preamble is a necessary evil. This is more for reasons of love than for technical reasons. It is quite rude to go abroad without even learning 'please' and 'thank you' in the local language, so the theologian who crashes into this space having not spent a polite amount of time learning vocabulary is like the ghastly caricature of the Britisher abroad: just speak louder and more slowly, and they are bound to understand you. But if a theologian is so because of their commitment to the God of love, who made humankind in his image, being rude to others should not be a deliberate policy. I will therefore use this introductory section to set out the basic grammar of doing theology in this space. To do so, I will have to revisit what theology is, and get technical about theological types, before we can return to the practicalities of doing theology about consumerism.

So, what is theology, and how would you spot a good one? To answer this question, I conducted a macro analysis of those theologians who have attempted to map this terrain within the fashionable genre of theological taxonomy. An economist would approve of this approach, because it essentially averages out a lot of theologians, to establish some generic means.

Theologians generally hate this approach, because it does violence to the particular. But that assumes that what I am doing is stirring together a bunch of theologians in a pot to create a bland stew that none of them would recognize. Instead, I am lurking in the bushes with my binoculars, watching how theologians behave. And what I have noticed is that the distracting glamour of their various spots and stripes obscures some essential similarities and differences. In hovering above these larger patterns, it becomes clear where public theology has often failed, and where we might then search for a better approach. One theologian who would approve of my approach is Avery Dulles, who has argued that models in general are peculiarly appropriate in theology, because their own inexactitude mirrors the necessarily provisional nature of statements about divine mysteries, and that a range of them should be deployed for mutual correction (Dulles 2002, pp. 2, 10f., 16). This approach will generate two macro models of theological type, from which to derive some criteria for a good – or at the very least, polite – theology about economics and consumerism.

From the vantage point of the topographer's helicopter, theologians are revealed to look either at theology about belief, or theology about itself. I have called these primary types Worldview theology and Etiquette theology. The next chapters will examine each in turn.

But first, a note on terminology. The language of typology and taxonomy, borrowed from botany and zoology, suggests absolute categories and scientific exactitude. In the field of theology, these categories can only function metaphorically. Yoder, who uses the notion of a typology to arrange the varieties of religious pacifism, differentiates between 'monolithically' logical typologies, which might resemble their scientific cousins, and those typologies which have fuzzier boundaries, but which ask useful 'typing questions' that point up similarities and differences. This leads him to draw a distinction between types and motifs. For him, 'typing' is the creation of a mutually exclusive and collectively exhaustive logical categorization, where, as in zoology, types fit neatly. 'Motifs' on the other hand are incomplete themes or 'accents' that stand side by side with other motifs awaiting revision (Yoder in Stassen *et al.* 1996, pp. 45, 48f.). This latter sense, which will be employed here, accommodates the caveat applied to type by Niebuhr who, after Weber and Jung, reminds the unwary typologist that no one person or group ever conforms completely to type, claiming to have persisted with his own only because of typology's ability to call to attention 'the continuity and significance of the great motifs that appear and reappear in the long wrestling of Christians' (Niebuhr 1956, p. 44). Yoder draws a distinction between a typology (how many types and how do they differ), a topology (placing the types on a map) and a taxonomy (describing the types within an overarching order or framework). While the sources consulted adopt a range of labels for their segmentation, Yoder's language of typology, topology and taxonomy will be used throughout for consistency, with the selected typologies being arranged topologically to derive taxonomic criteria (Yoder 1992, p. 12).

Also, a note on method. The authors of the types chosen make uneven bedfellows, and the exercise will inevitably be distracting to those who are familiar with the attendant theology of the typologists considered. Nonetheless, the contention is that their typologies can legitimately be considered in relative and artificial isolation, to create the 'laboratory' conditions required to discern any commonality between them. This treatment mirrors the exercise of typing itself, which requires the isolation of factors in order to discern patterns. While any typology springs from a given context, the function of type is to be generic, so this exercise also tests the typologies for robustness against the field. In comparing typologies, the generalities between them will be 'rolled up' to establish high-level criteria for healthy theology. It may be that the typologies readily available for critique are not the only or the best ones in existence. However, the emerging topology can be used to surface taxonomic categories, on the basis that the family resemblances between the typologies may be predictive of their missing relatives.

But beware: as Wittgenstein would point out, I am calling the rules of this language game, and they may not be your rules. Feel free to heed Pirsig's warning and apply your own categories, if mine do not help you:

> There is a knife moving here. A very deadly one, an intellectual scalpel so swift and so sharp you sometimes don't see it moving. You get the illusion that all those parts are just there and are being named as they exist. But they can be named quite differently and organized quite differently depending on how the knife moves. (Pirsig 1974, p. 81)

2

Worldview Theology

The first type cluster is termed the 'worldview' group, because its members tend to press theology into the service of a particular mission or view of reality. This cluster is a bit eclectic, but the types represented in it are characterized by an attempt to explain how God and the world relate, through different accounts of reality.

H. Richard Niebuhr

Cheat sheet

H. Richard Niebuhr, whose elder brother was also a famous theologian, wrote his classic book *Christ and Culture* in 1951. In it, he sets out a scheme to describe how Christianity tends to respond to culture, identifying five prevailing viewpoints (see below). These range from Christ against Culture, which is a rejection of culture, through a spectrum of engagement towards Christ the Transformer of Culture, in which society is converted and redeemed through the active participation of Christians. This scheme is a popular one, as it explains the familiar range of reactions to cultural phenomena like consumerism, from those who avoid the mainstream economy on grounds of conscience, to those who create business models like fairtrade in order to make the market more Christ-like. Niebuhr himself seems to have favoured this last approach as representing the most appropriate Christian response to modernity.

Chronologically, H. Richard Niebuhr's famous typology is the first to fit into the Worldview category. Originating in his 1949 Austin lectures, it has five categories, relating to the relative positionings of Christ and culture, by which he means the world, civilization, or 'the total process of human activity and the total result of such activity'. Having examined the various debates through history about the nature of Christ and the nature of culture and how they relate, he identifies these five categories as typical Christian answers to the 'problem' of Christ and culture. His types are: Christ against Culture, Christ of Culture, Christ above Culture, Christ and Culture in Paradox, and Christ the Transformer of Culture (Niebuhr 1956, p. 32). He sees them as recurring so often in different eras and societies that they seem to be 'less the product of historical conditioning than of the nature of the problem itself and the meanings of its terms'. Of his five Christ and Culture types, one type 'agrees', one 'opposes', and three are a subgroup that mediates between Christ and culture, variously combining these two 'authorities' (p. 40).

The first, Christ against Culture, was historically exemplified by the exhortation to leave the world behind, for example by entering a closed religious order. Niebuhr regards this type as epitomizing the classic 'either–or' decision, where Christ is seen to be offering a stark choice between himself or culture, with culture being seen as standing in opposition to Christ. In this type, loyalty is owed solely to Christ, as demonstrated by members of the early Church, and is an expression of confidence in the love of God. For Niebuhr, other examples of this type would be Tertullian and Tolstoy, and all of those monastics, mystics, sects or movements like the Mennonites or the Quakers who kept themselves separate to avoid taint and corruption. In welcoming the purity of this position, Niebuhr notes that all Christians have to experience this withdrawal and renunciation to some extent, to avoid their faith becoming a 'utilitarian device for the attainment of personal prosperity or public peace'. In critiquing this position, he notes that it is impossible truly to separate humanity from culture – history, ideas, language – and that this perspective neglects the immanence of God in the whole of creation (pp. 40, 45, 47, 68).

His second type, Christ of Culture, emphasizes the agreement between Christ and culture, as exemplified in modern efforts to show democracy or civilization as evidence of God's purposes being worked out through contemporary cultural institutions. In this type, Niebuhr says that Jesus will often appear as the hero of human cultural history, confirming what is best and guiding civilization towards culmination. As part of culture, in this type Christ represents a social heritage that must be transmitted and conserved. Niebuhr sees this type as being dominant in Protestant liberalism and epitomized by Abelard. Using and thereby conforming to the categories of culture ('religion', 'ethics' and so on), it seeks to harmonize Christ and culture, regarding the world as a training ground for the world to come. Niebuhr numbers John Locke, Kant, Thomas Jefferson, Hegel, Emerson, Albrecht Ritschl and, to an extent, Schleiermacher among this type. With its incarnational and utopian feel, he sums it up in the epithet 'the Fatherhood of God and the Brotherhood of Man' in that Christianity in this type is a sort of über-philosophy, being the crowning of the Enlightenment project and the illumination of the Constitutions of its new States. While this perspective appears differently as differing elements of culture and history are 'baptized' by different groups, throughout, the habit remains to identify Christ with whatever a given group sees as their noblest ideals, philosophies and institutions. This type – famous for its 'relevance' – has been of great service in communicating Christianity to culture down the centuries. Babel-like, it helps different people to hear the gospel in their own language, and as a type is embodied in the example of St Paul. Niebuhr notes that, while this chameleon Christ may become relativistic, it can offend culture by colonizing it, and fall foul of the theologians by cherry-picking gobbets that speak to a current preoccupation, thereby distorting the totality of Christ. For him, if the first type privileges revelation, this type privileges reason, attracting an equal charge of bias and rendering itself susceptible to critique based on the 'irrationality' of belief in Christ and divine grace (pp. 41, 84ff., 101, 103, 108f.).

Like the second type, the third, Christ above Culture, regards Christ as the culmination of culture. As the first of Niebuhr's median types, this type goes further, however, in regarding Christ as 'discontinuous as well as continuous' with culture, such that culture may lead people towards Christ but that a 'great leap' is nonetheless needed if people are to reach him. For this type, true culture is not possible unless 'Christ enters into life from above with gifts which human aspiration has not envisioned, and which human effort cannot attain unless he relates men to a supernatural society and a new value-center'. For Niebuhr, this type is exemplified in the writings of Justin Martyr, Clement of Alexandria and Aquinas. These 'synthesists' have a 'both-and' view of Christ and culture, resting on a recognition that Christ is fully human and fully divine. Adherents of this type hold that one must be good in accordance with the best cultural standards, but that there is a stage of existence beyond the morally respectable life. Such an existence, in which life is lived in love wholly for its own sake, can only be attained beyond this world, but culture in this one prepares us for it by helping us to realize our God-given potential. While it cannot do so adequately, or make us deserving of ultimate happiness in the next life, it can make our hearts receptive to any such gift from God. Niebuhr would however critique the synthesists on the grounds that 'culture' is not fixed, so it is not clear which culture is the one with which humanity should engage in its moral quest. He feels that this problem leads the type into cultural conservatism and towards unhealthy hierarchies about which sorts of cultural life might be most favoured, and fails adequately to address the problem of 'radical evil' in the world (pp. 42, 120, 127, 132ff., 145ff., 148).

The fourth type, Christ and Culture in Paradox, recognizes that both Christ and culture have authority and accepts the opposition between them. This sets up life as a dilemma in which both contrasting authorities must simultaneously be obeyed. The tension between them cannot be resolved in this world, but obedience to both is nonetheless required. It is not as approving of culture as are types two and three, neither is it as opposed to culture as is type one. Typified for Niebuhr by Luther, this type sees humanity as being subject to two moralities and as a citizen of two worlds: 'in the *polarity* and *tension* of Christ and culture life must be lived precariously and sinfully in the hope of a justification which lies beyond history'. Adherents of the fourth type, like the third, have a 'both-and' view of Christ and culture, but the 'dualists' differ from the 'synthesists' in their view that Christ and culture cannot be combined. Thus, their 'train-tracks' of Christ and culture do not converge but run in parallel. Given the reality of sin, the miracle of God's grace 'is the action of reconciliation that reaches out across the no-man's-land of the historic war of men against God'. Faith is not human-made but God-given, and culture, like all human work, is fundamentally corrupt. All attempts to domesticate God in culture, through reason, law and religion, are depraved, and these feeble attempts at power are evidence of godlessness. This type therefore agrees with the 'Christ against Culture' type that culture is 'sick unto death'. However, this type accepts this paradox rather than retreating from it, because the dualist recognizes that they belong to culture and are sustained by God's initiative within it. While for this type culture may not be a route to Christ, its transformation is nevertheless necessary as a bulwark against the worst excesses of sin, even if such attempts at transformation are in vain. For the dualists, the key paradoxes between Christ and culture are those of law and grace, and divine wrath and mercy. While for Niebuhr this type appears more as a motif than a system in theology, he glimpses it in the writings of Paul and Marcion, and particularly in Luther's doctrine of the Two Kingdoms. He also sees modern developments of it in the dualisms of church/state, faith/reason, and so on. In critiquing this position, 'a report of experience rather than a plan of campaign', Niebuhr praises its honesty and dynamism but sees its danger as an antinomian counsel of despair, accidentally providing the rationale for a fatalistic refusal to resist temptation by eliding the practical difference between sinful obedience and sinful disobedience. Like type three, it tends towards cultural conservatism as a logical consequence of perceiving culture – and in particular government – as a restraining dyke against sin rather than a positive agency for good (pp. 43, 151, 156–7, 185, 188).

His final type, Niebuhr calls the 'conversionist' solution: Christ the Transformer of Culture. Like types one and four, this type recognizes the fallen nature of humanity as appearing in and being transmitted through culture, but, instead of advocating withdrawal or patience, this last type sees Christ as the converter of humanity in and not apart from culture, 'for there is no nature without culture and no turning of men from self and idols to God save in society'. While recognizing with the dualists the reality of sin, the conversionists are more positive and hopeful towards culture, putting the doctrines of creation/incarnation and redemption/atonement on a more equal footing, such that human culture has always been subject to God's ordering action. Additionally, the conversionists do not conflate creation with the Fall in the way that the dualists tend to, instead maintaining a clear separation between God's action (creation) and human action (the Fall) (pp. 43, 193ff.). Thus culture is perverted but not essentially evil, and so might be converted through the spiritual transformation of humanity in the present as well as in the future. As represented by the classical theological theme of perfection, this type holds that the moral virtues developed in culture can be converted by love, such that human 'spirits with an animal nature' might turn from sin back to a state of union with God. For Niebuhr, this type is demonstrated by the Gospel of John, which 'converts' Hellenistic motifs into Christian ones. It is exemplified by Augustine's conversion and many of his writings, and by Calvin, especially in his treatment of vocation. The conversionist type is particularly illustrated in the thought of F. D. Maurice, with his rejection of the dualism that regards the flesh as essentially sinful, and his optimism about perfection being a present possibility. That Niebuhr refrains from offering critical comment on this final type may suggest it is his favourite (p. 222, quoting F. D. Maurice, pp. 196ff., 108, 217ff., 218ff.; see Stassen *et al.* 1996, p. 191).

Before Niebuhr's typology became a classic, it famously attracted strong criticism from John Howard Yoder. His criticism, written in 1958, was initially circulated informally. It remained unpublished until 1996, when it appeared with Niebuhr's previously unpublished essay of 1942 in which he had first laid out his Christ and culture typology (see Stassen *et al.* 1996). First, Yoder struggled to slot theologians into Niebuhr's scheme, which made him instantly suspicious of it. He also took issue with Niebuhr's thinly veiled preference for the *Transformer* type over the others, judging Niebuhr by his own view that 'the typologist needs to remember that he is not constructing a value scale. His enterprise is directed neither towards explanation nor evaluation, but towards understanding and appreciation' (Stassen *et al.* 1996, p. 16). Additionally, Yoder charges Niebuhr with equivocation and inaccuracy in his use of 'culture' and 'Christ' as categories. In his view, the former is used too monolithically, and he takes issue with the theological accuracy of the picture Niebuhr paints of the latter (Stassen *et al.* 1996, pp. 54–6, 59–61). His criticisms of Niebuhr's neglect of the role of the Church and his treatment of the Trinity relate more to Niebuhr's theological argument for his favoured type than to his typology per se, but Yoder uses them to throw into question the usefulness of any model that neglects theological realities in favour of what he sees as a false logical integrity (Stassen *et al.* 1996, on the Trinity, pp. 61ff.; and Stassen's reply, p. 141; on the role of the Church, pp. 74ff.).

A number of key typological questions or principles may be winnowed from this critique. First, there is the question of whether or not a typology is an a priori logical device, and to what extent it corresponds with an empirical reality. This point was emphasized by Yoder in noticing how few theologians seemed to be accommodated by Niebuhr's typology. Related to this is the extent to which the variables selected are terms or concepts that are discrete and agreed, given the consternation that greeted Niebuhr's use of the categories of Christ and culture. A further consideration is to what extent the typology is, as Niebuhr himself recommends, a device that offers understanding not evaluation. Whether or not a typology could ever be 'impartial' is a moot point, but Yoder's frustration with Niebuhr arises largely from his perceived dishonesty rather than from his partiality, suggesting that typologists might profit from making plain their underlying assumptions or biases. Finally, the criteria for the evaluation of any typology are important. Apart from the practical 'test' of face validity applied by Yoder, there are the theological 'tests' that have been applied to Niebuhr, in scrutinizing the theology implied in his typology and its argumentation, and biases or gaps such as the role of the Church in this instance.

One could argue that to start and stop with this typology would be adequate in examining as 'cultural' an activity such as consumerism. However, a consideration of this typology alongside other such constructions provides a richer basis for comparison than could be achieved by looking at any one typology on its own.

John B. Cobb

Cheat sheet

Born to missionaries in Japan, John B. Cobb is best known as the champion of process theology and has also been a long-time campaigner on environmental ethics. He coined his typology in 1959, because he was worried that theology had become more about humankind than it was about God. To get back to basics, he identified the three great properties of God, and described the theologies that would emerge from an emphasis on each. Absolutist theology has a mystical flavour, because it tries hard to articulate something that is by definition unknowable. Personalistic theology uses the highest human attributes like consciousness and reason as cyphers for knowing God. Process theology wonders how God's goodness enters the world, so concentrates its efforts on describing these processes. Cobb's model starts to explore how we project our own interpretations on to God. The Jones typology develops this further, from an empirical base (see later). Both therefore serve to remind us that all talk about God risks saying more about us than human language ever could about the divine.

Writing in 1959, Cobb established a typology that was intended to redress the imbalance he had noticed creeping into theology whereby the emphasis seemed to be more on the 'doctrine of man' than the doctrine of God. For him, the two doctrines together comprise theology proper, but while theologies about human beings are illuminating, he was concerned that they were suffering from a variety of underlying 'unarticulated assumptions about the nature of God' (Cobb 1959, p. 183). His typology was therefore intended as a corrective, offering a way of thinking about the doctrine of God in particular. His typology examines the three 'characteristics' of God he sees as existing in tension, and which give rise to three contrasting theological emphases. His chosen characteristics as to the essential nature of God, without which the word 'God' would be inappropriate, are absoluteness, personality and goodness. These in turn produce his three types: Absolutist, Personalistic and Process theologies.

His Absolutist type starts from the position that God is utterly free from all that limits human beings, such that he in no way changes or is changed, and exists outside time. This gives rise to a theology that emphasizes our inability to articulate the changelessness of God except through the medium of language, which is too human and changeable a device to be able to be literal. This means that all positive affirmations about God can only be symbolic, and that a posteriori arguments for God's existence are similarly suspect and provisional. Adherents of this type of theology may be mystical or Gnostic, because for Cobb our lack of knowledge and our transience in the face of God's absolute reality and timelessness renders humanity somehow less real or possibly unreal, pointing towards a salvation that is out of this body and out of this world: 'the "real" self which must be timeless, cannot be the empirical self and cannot ultimately be differentiated from timeless reality generally or from God' (p. 188). This position has something in common with Niebuhr's Christ against Culture type, in that it leaves the world behind. In critiquing this position, Cobb notes the contradiction between it and a biblical account showing God purposefully acting in time, and he notes the problem of justifying religious symbols in a worldview that regards them as fundamentally illusory. The most serious challenge, however, is the philosophical one. If God is absolute yet historically revealed, faith is required to trump reason in order to resolve this paradox. Cobb concludes: 'If then faith must affirm strict contradictions in one area of thought over against reason, all use of reason even to define its own limits would appear suspect from the point of view of faith, and no limit seems in principle possible to the claims of faith, however obviously they may contradict human experience and scientific knowledge' (p. 189).

In contrast, Cobb's Personalist type attributes to God those higher characteristics present in human experience such as consciousness, intelligence and purpose. These similarities allow the believer to address God with the confidence of being in communion with a spirit that is vastly superior to, but somehow reminiscent of, ourselves. That these are ascribed characteristics based on human experience of them Cobb sees as inevitably assigning some degree of temporality to God, in that any concept of these characteristics that was outside of time would be so 'wholly other' as to make it otiose. The Personalists therefore differ from the Absolutists in this key aspect of temporality. This 'both-and' position is rather like Niebuhr's mediating Christ and culture types. Cobb's logical critique of this position is similar to that of a critique of realism, in that there is no proof either of the literal existence of God or humanity such that it can be claimed with certainty that they may hold traits in common. That this uncertainty requires faith to be held tentatively pending proof renders it precarious, unless it succumbs to the mysticism and relativism of the empirical argument from experience. Moreover, doctrines such as the Trinity and the incarnation are unlikely to make sense for Personalists, making them unorthodox, and they have no defence against the problem of evil. These challenges inevitably push this type either towards an insistence that this is in some way the best of all possible worlds, or to a position that God's power is in some way limited (pp. 189–92).

Cobb introduces his third type, Process theology, to answer the charge that: 'if God is no more than an unknowable "wholly other" or an inference for which some probability is claimed, then man may be excused for turning elsewhere'. The result is an approach that defines God as 'the trans-human source of human good', such that goodness is God's distinctive characteristic and evil cannot therefore be the expression of his will and power. This means that the task of theology is to describe those processes whereby God brings about good in order to indicate how humans might fruitfully relate to them (pp. 184, 192). Where it seeks to 'baptize' latent evidence of God's work in the world, this type might resemble Niebuhr's *Christ of Culture*. Cobb's major critique of this position is that it does not satisfy the demands of personal communion because it fails on the same grounds as those previously, in that its appeal to 'good' is philosophically vexed. Moreover, in this view:

> It seems that God must be either a scattered group of events connected only by abstract resemblances or else he must be the abstract pattern exemplified by such events. In the former case we may desire that similar events occur again, and, while they are occurring, we may submit ourselves to their influence; but it would seem that they would be regarded inevitably as means to our ends rather than as objects of religious commitment. In the latter case they can awaken only the kinds of attitude appropriate to abstract possibilities. In other words, it seems doubtful whether God as characterized in this system can in fact function as object of supreme devotion for more than a small number of persons, except when associations with other uses of the word God not warranted by this approach are transferred to it. (p. 193)

In proposing these three types, Cobb traces the Absolutist perspective back to Greek intellectual influence and the Personalistic perspective to Scripture, noting that these two set up what was for Kierkegaard the supreme paradox of faith. He regards continental Europe as favouring the Absolutist approach, America as favouring the Personalist approach, and Britain as occupying a position somewhere in between. Writing in 1959, he forecast in America a move towards the Process approach, although it had not then in his view taken off abroad. In offering his typology, he is careful to note that in spite of their difficulties all three of the approaches 'solve problems'. He is however keen to improve their mutual dialogue by offering 'a sharp delineation of their opposed presuppositions [that] should conduce to intelligibility' (pp. 185, 194).

Cobb was of course instrumental in developing and progressing process theology in America but, as with Niebuhr, it is his typology itself and not his theology that will be pressed into service here. Apart from Cobb's own critique, a presenting issue is his emphasis on God at the expense of any commentary on the particularity of Christianity, rendering his position essentially theist. He justifies this by arguing that while all theology must be 'bipolar', by which he means centring on a doctrine of the human and a doctrine of God, he regards subjects of Christology, soteriology and ecclesiology as 'methodologically secondary', because they rest on assumptions about God that need to be surfaced first.

Paul Jones

Cheat sheet

In the 1980s Paul Jones conducted a very detailed multi-media analysis of seminarians and pastors to find out what they believed. Using legends, music, stories and art, he identified five distinct theological 'worlds' (see below). Each has a presenting issue and a divine resolution, so they describe how believers self-identify and what kind of God they seek to save them. For example, in the world where the believer feels empty, they seek a God who promises fulfilment. The Jones typology is unique and tricky: does using 'evidence' in this way just hand victory to those atheists who would argue that religion is entirely a therapeutic but delusional anthropological construct? Of course, as our children know from *The Gruffalo*, even if you make something up, it might also exist. Jones had five children – all girls – and is now a Trappist monk.

In 1989, Jones identified five 'theological worlds' within Christianity. Each world is a style of meaning-making about human existence, wagered on God, which acts as an orientation for life. Based on extensive research and experimentation, albeit in a solely Protestant context, in each case they are characterized by a differing *obsessio* (dilemma) attuned to a contrasting *epiphania* (resolution). Jones' typology is interesting in that it is the first to be considered that relies on empirical socio-psychological evidence and not on a priori categorization (Jones 1989, pp. 13, 18ff.).

Jones developed his Worlds model through his research into the 'theologizing process' of several theologians. He defines this as 'the process of identifying, nurturing, forging, or re-forging one's impulsing logic as identifiable narrative, whether magnetized by imagery of battlefield or of cottage' (p. 235). He spent five years experimenting with his model, with over 200 Protestant seminary students and about 100 pastors. His findings were further tested in one-to-one sessions with non-clergy professionals, then re-tested on further students and pastors and converted into an inventory to help people to identify the world to which they belonged. Believing that 'the aesthetic enterprise distils metaphors that promise a World', he triangulated his typology with sets of paintings, music, literature, mythology and images to reach a deeper illustration of each type. His conclusion is that the 'natives' in each world will find dialogue with 'foreigners' frustrating, and that this leads to conflict of both a secular and theological kind (p. 24).

His first world is called Separation and Reunion, in which authenticity is questing in the face of an overwhelming cosmos cloaked in mystery. Characterized by Romeo and Juliet as its tragic form on the one hand and Odysseus as its comedic form on the other, its worldview is about alienation and longing, such that its spirituality is about contemplation and its theology is about coming home. Christ is therefore a Revealer or Evoker, a guide to take the *Alien* to the place of reunion and to reveal the truth. His representative modern theology to illustrate this rather Gnostic world is neo-liberalism, as exemplified for him by Tillich and Dostoevsky (pp. 20ff., 42, 45ff., 121ff.).

In the second world, of Conflict and Vindication, the central dilemma concerns history as chaos, characterized in tragedy by Beowulf and in comedy by Don Quixote. This worldview is outraged by Fate, and feelings of oppression drive rebellion and conflict to deny it dominion. The *Warrior* therefore seeks a Christ who will be the Liberator or Messiah, and who will 'change the truth' by triumphing over death. Spirituality is therefore about intercession, and theology is preoccupied with a thirst for justice, making God take sides to guarantee a victory. Liberation theology, as rooted in Barth, would be Jones' representative theology for this world (pp. 20ff., 42, 57ff., 137ff.).

The *Outcast* lives in the third world, of Emptiness and Fulfilment, struggling with the possibilities for the unfulfilled self. Characterized by Hamlet or Parsifal, this world needs Christ to be a role model, and theology is about belonging. Being a more passive form of world two, in this world the outcast feels the ache of impotence and worthlessness, and has only their own lack of perceived significance to blame – they are invisible, somehow empty and not there. The task of theology is therefore to provide the tools for the Outcast to 'become', often involving a journey of self-discovery through meditation and suffering towards wholeness. Jones selects process theology to illustrate this world (pp. 20, 22, 43, 70ff., 148f.).

The fourth world is characterized by Condemnation and Forgiveness, whose path passes through 'the valley of the shadow of guilt' and is characterized by Faustus or King Lear. Born into indebtedness and marred by original sin, the *Fugitive* is damned by his conscience to be more than his animal nature, and is seeking expiation. While the world conspires against integrity, there is a restlessness for morality within it. The diseased soul needs the threat of hell to avoid giving in to its Freudian nature, but there is no hope without a confession of the need for atonement, and epiphany comes through brokenness. Christ is the Redeemer who will reprieve the Fugitive through adoption. Theology is centred on the cross, and is likely to be rich with themes of human waywardness, demonic forces and the divine gift of grace. Barth is also used by Jones to illustrate the theology of this world, which he terms neo-orthodoxy (pp. 20, 22, 43, 81ff., 166ff.).

The final world, Suffering and Endurance, wrestles with an awareness that living means persisting on the edge of absurdity. Its tragic form is characterized by Oedipus, with its comedy being the endurance of Sisyphus. The *Victim/Refugee* feels overwhelmed by an incomprehensible world, where death is the only certainty. Being a more passive form of world four, suffering is central to this world, and is morally indiscriminate. However, through suffering dying becomes less alien and threatening, and suffering is the refiner's fire that makes the victim stronger. In this world the dignity of enduring is paramount, and the wisdom it brings is its own reward. Silence is the best response to the inevitability of life, and some solace may come from those who suffer alongside, sitting it out, waiting and lasting. If there is a God in this world, Christ is the suffering servant and the companion, and theology is likely to centre on themes of survival and integrity. For Jones, existentialism is the intellectual illustration of this world, as seen in the theology of Kierkegaard (pp. 20, 22, 43, 97ff., 180ff.).

Jones' typology essentially answers the question about why people believe, and in doing so suggests what they believe too. In the UK, Tim Jenkins' ethnographic studies have asked a similar question, about why people go to church. His findings are suggestive of another kind of typological split. His studies show that the underlying social motivation for church attendance is to do with 'respectability', which comprises 'inner restraint and outward reputation', established either via 'public good' in the mainstream or by 'private honour' towards the fringes. While both might be achieved by the 'division of labour' of occasional or associated attendance, the style of church will tend to attract one type or the other, with those whose respectability comes from the 'private honour' end of the spectrum most likely to make their own informal spiritual arrangements. While there are a huge number of 'church' typing books, whether they sort on sociological, cultural or churchmanship lines, Jenkins' distinction is a particularly interesting one in a UK context (Jenkins in Guest *et al.*, 2004).

Returning to Jones, in looking at his typology one is struck with its resonance with psychological typology, and particularly the work of William Schutz. In 1958, Schutz developed a psychometric instrument to help people to understand their interpersonal orientation towards others, originally in the context of the US submariner community. His instrument synthesized a number of psychological approaches to examine three 'fundamental' types of interpersonal behaviour and what drives them. He suggests that, interpersonally, we will normally display those behaviours which we would like to attract back from others, so that each behavioural type has an 'expressed' and 'wanted' face. His behaviours are inclusion, control and affection, and they are driven by three matching preoccupations. Inclusion is driven by feelings related to significance, control by feelings of competence, and affection by feelings of lovability (Kendall and McHenry 1997, pp. 1–8; Ryan 1989).

Comparing Schutz with the typology of Jones, it seems that his first two worlds arise from a psychological preoccupation with competence. In the first world, the journey is towards enlightenment, such that the Alien finds the truth about the world, becoming 'competent' in it as a result. This suggests a leaning towards the kinds of structures of control that suggest competence, so Aliens may gravitate towards formal institutions that provide meaning, or promise itineraries of discovery to accompany them on their quest; and to be seeking gurus, teachers or leaders who can help. This hypothesis would resonate with Jones' analysis of Christ as the Revealer for this world. In the second world, the Warrior subdues the world around him, resonating with Schutz's notion of expressed control, as a way of asserting the self over and against a recalcitrant world to feel competent (potent and victorious) over it. In the third world, the Outcast feels like they are melting away, which in Schutz's terms refers to feelings of insignificance and of being overlooked, by being denied inclusion by others. The Outcast longs for this inclusion, wanting it from others but feeling unable to offer it themselves, so is locked into a downward spiral by never feeling included enough to exhibit the kinds of including behaviours they want to attract back in return. The fourth world recalls Schutz's notion of wanted affection, in that the Fugitive wants to be considered lovable in spite of the vicissitudes of their nature, as epitomized in this world's yearning for divine grace and forgiveness. Schutz does not have a preoccupation that neatly maps to the final world, in which the Victim just soldiers on, except that a score of zero across all of Schutz's categories might cohere with this passive profile.

However, this framework suggests that there are likely to be at least two missing worlds in Jones' typology. While Schutz examines the range of interpersonal preoccupations only, there remain two such expressions that are not yet covered in Jones' worlds. These are the expression of inclusion and the expression of affection. Were there to be a world which was characterized by the expression of inclusion, the *Mother* might reach out to her fellow humans to nurture them, honouring their significance as part of creation. Theology in this mode would be about co-creation and the realization of human potential within the divine order. Similarly, were there to be a world characterized by the expression of affection, the *Lover* might cherish her fellow humans, regardless of what they deserve, and theology would be about unconditional love and the inherent goodness of creation. While these additional worlds are something of a conceptual construct, they serve to highlight a bias towards passivity even in Jones' more active worlds, and possibly towards stereotypical masculinity, perhaps via bias in his sample (Jones is silent on the gender split in it). Thus they suggest a particular anthropology implicit in his model which may repay further examination. This potential bias is also suggested by the analysis in Christopher Booker's *Seven Basic Plots* about recurring themes in the world's classic stories. While Jones' worlds arguably map onto Booker's categories of the Quest, Overcoming the Monster, Rebirth, Voyage and Return, and Tragedy, his more positive categories of Rags to Riches and Comedy are not so evidently paralleled.

Jones' unusual model serves to suggest the importance again of a clear underlying construct, regardless of the persuasive nature of any empirical evidence that supports it. The danger with 'sophistry and illusion' is that it can have no basis in fact, but the danger of 'evidence' is that it imprisons knowledge in the dataset of the day and the age. A further danger that arises from the use of any psychological typography within theology is that it can lead to a determinism that risks denying free will, as well as privileging the epistemology favoured by that discipline to the exclusion of all other categories.

Wesley Kort

Cheat sheet

Another American, Wesley Kort, hails from Duke, and identifies three different strands of theological discourse. Either we talk about God in the Prophetic mode, the Priestly mode or the Sapiential mode. The first, his X-type, is concerned with other-world matters. The second, his Y-type, is concerned with how these other-world matters enter the world. His Z-type is concerned with the human condition. Interestingly, Kort sees these categories as mutually exclusive. He called his 1988 typology *Bound to Differ* because he wanted to be honest about the inevitability of conflict in religious discourse. Where religious views are held both strongly and differently, there can be no faithful agreement. But at least if we are aware about the fault lines, we can be realistic about what is possible in any kind of ecumenical setting.

Published in 1992, the most recent of the first four typologies is Kort's three varieties of Christian theology. He starts by identifying six theological topics which in his view form the standard agenda of theological enquiry: theology, Christology, ecclesiology, anthropology, soteriology and eschatology. He notes that theologians talk about all of these topics but from 'differing bases' which yield predictable results. He identifies these bases as being three discrete 'discourses', identified through the conflict that necessarily arises from the differences between them. The bases arise from three 'meaning effects' in theology, which he calls X – other-world matters, Y – how these are mediated to/in this world, and Z – the human condition in this world. For Kort, a discrete theological discourse is a set of strategies to establish and defend the domination of one of the meaning effects over the other two (Kort 1992, pp. ix, 48ff.). All three have to be there for a discourse to be 'theological', but the split in emphasis between them varies. These three 'meaning effects' produce his three 'types' or discourses by each being pre-eminent in turn:

> The two points must be made with equal emphasis: (1) in any theological discourse all three kinds of signifiers will be present; and (2) in any theological discourse one of them will dominate the other two and deform them toward itself. (p. 50)

For Kort, theological argumentation is not about individual theological topics, such as God or sin, but their proper *relation* one to another. Theologies that arise as a reaction to a particular political topic are therefore mistakenly partial and neglectful of this primary question as to fundamental relations. So for Kort, theology consists of three versions or schema concerning the 'rightness' of a particular set of relations (p. 122). He then sees conflict as a causal factor in theology, as well as the inevitable by-product of it, in that the act of defending and maintaining one emphasis over the other two necessarily requires their denigration, reinforced through narrative and ritual (pp. 53, 134). This produces Kort's mutually exclusive typology, such that, if X is pre-eminent, the theology will prioritize other-world matters (the Prophetic type); if Y, it will prioritize mediation (the Priestly type); and if Z, it will prioritize the human condition (the Sapiential type) (pp. 50, 54ff.). As well as explaining the inevitability of religious conflict, Kort uses his typology to explain why resolution or any type of ecumenism is impossible, because the policing of these discourse boundaries within Christianity necessarily extends to the policing of external boundaries with non-Christians and with the secular world, creating inevitable conflict at each frontier (pp. 127ff.). For him, an overarching ecumenical theology cannot exist, in that any attempt to identify such a scheme would result in hopeless abstraction. Battle can therefore only be suspended if spokespersons of all three kinds agree to defer to some other discourse (for instance, free speech, or the need for a united response to a common threat), although Kort thinks this compromise yields description rather than theology. He further notes the general theological tension arising from 'the immunity of Christian theological discourses from and their vulnerability to general language categories and theories', as well as the tension between their dependence on and independence from the very dynamics of discourse (p. 62; pp. 6f.).

In brief, Prophetic discourses have as their 'hidden premise' the 'primacy in power, meaning, worth, or being of what lies beyond human understanding and control'. They are characteristically 'theological' in style, using the language of transcendence (the supernatural, the divine, the eternal, and so on) with care, and are loath to compromise other-worldly matters by domesticating them. This makes them wary of 'particular forms or occasions by which the divine is accessible to human approach' and of empiricism in general, because it relies on this-world analysis of human entities and events (p. 69).

In contrast, Priestly discourses assume that 'forms or occasions' of divine presence in the world provide the starting point and the primary focus of theology. For Y theologians, what can be said about the world or about God must logically derive from such 'forms and occasions' where they meet. In Christianity, the primary focus of such theologians is Christology, the Bible or the Church, as representing tangible 'data' about God and the world (pp. 85ff.).

The Sapiential discourse starts instead with 'the needs and potentials of the human world'. Abhorring the 'life-denying obscurantism and privatization' of the other two types, Z theologians will naturally gravitate towards theological anthropology and soteriology, and make particular use of the Wisdom literature. Within this type, Z theologians may differently value the world, being optimistic or pessimistic in orientation, and Kort sees them displaying three different foci: a focus on the natural world, a focus on spirituality, or a focus on human diversity and how best to reconcile human communities (pp. 101–4).

Kort is unusual among these typologists for his insistence on the inevitability of conflict. Jones admits the possibility but does not make a feature of it, and conflict is not central to the understanding of the types of Niebuhr or Cobb. While Kort is rather dramatic on this point, he is supported by a compelling weight of scholarship regarding the theoretical inevitability of conflict arising from religious differences. Apart from theories of mimetic desire, research on interpersonal differences and in-group/outgroup social identity behaviour suggests that the more ontological the difference, the more it is likely to be perceived as a personal attack and to provoke an emotional reaction. This reaction affects the cognitive faculties, making 'reason' harder, such that escalation is a natural outcome. This perhaps makes him more realistic than the other typologists in understanding what is at stake when one articulates or creates a worldview typology (Savage and Boyd-MacMillan 2007, pp. 16–19, 111–14).

In some ways, Kort's typology includes those of Niebuhr and Cobb. His 'other-world matters' or Prophetic type is like Cobb's Absolutist mode and Niebuhr's 'Christ against Culture'. His 'how these are mediated to/in this world' or Priestly type is like Niebuhr's median types with their combinations of the divine imperatives of Christ and nature, and resonates with Cobb's notion of the Personalist type. Kort's 'human condition in this world' or Sapiential type is similar to Cobb's Process type, and akin to Niebuhr's 'Christ of Culture' type. Jones' typology would probably fit into Kort's Sapiential type, with its emphasis on the human condition. The parallels are inexact, but that they resemble each other may suggest a harmonizing logic for 'worldview' typing in theology.

Worldview Synthesis

Niebuhr's typology is often used as the exemplar of this way of describing theology, but the other taxonomists in the Worldview category add colour through their use of empirical data (Paul Jones), or ideas about the inevitability of conflict between contrasting theologies (Wesley Kort). Some start by defining God, using divine properties to frame theological priorities (John Cobb). Others examine the relationship between God and the world and use a preoccupation with aspects of this to derive theologies (Kort), or they start with an examination of the reported beliefs of individual Christians to surface immanent theological trends about the nature of the world (Jones). Niebuhr himself starts with Christ, and uses his relation to the world to frame his categories. Considered together, the various taxonomies of worldview theology split into three leanings or biases: God, Between and World. The three macro types are divided into those in which God is the chief concern, those in which the world is the chief concern, and those in which mediation between the two is the chief concern. In Niebuhr-speak, the God category is his Christ against Culture, the World category is his Christ of Culture, and the Between category comprises his three median types. In the context of Christian typology, Christ as the archetypal mediator is of particular relevance in the Between category. There is inevitable blurring across the three categories, but the family resemblances they bear to each other support this common underlying logic:

	God	Between	World
Kort	Prophetic	Priestly	Sapiential
Cobb	Absolutist	Personalist	Process
Niebuhr	Christ against Culture	Three Median Types	Christ of Culture
Jones			Five Worlds

An analysis of these worldview typologies suggests that typing efforts should observe a number of protocols. First, the type labels used should be as precise as possible to prevent confusion. Theological or philosophical terminology may assist, provided it follows standard usage. Whether the type displays itself as an a priori logical device or an empirically wrought construct, in each case the underlying beliefs and assumptions informing the segmentation – whether theological, anthropological or cultural – should be clearly stated. As appropriate, the categories should be related to suitable evidence or examples to prove the concept. That Niebuhr himself seemed unable to offer a typology that aided understanding without offering evaluation suggests that as a criterion impartiality becomes subterfuge. However, this principle suggests that the typologist should at least be careful to state their intentions in developing their typology and the use to which it is to be put. Additionally, the type will need to demonstrate its credentials as a Christian typology or as a typology of theism in general, and to be clear about the sorts of truth-claims being made. For example, David Tracy has identified a range of standard verification models displayed in recent theologies, spanning the correspondence, coherence, experience, disclosure, praxis/transformation and consensus approaches to truth-claiming (Tracy 1981, pp. 62ff.). Where a typology borrows from a particular academic tradition (such as the social sciences), the typologist should be careful to note that tradition's assumptions throughout so as not to inherit unwitting bias. Lastly, the typologist should be careful about the scope for conflict that may arise in creating a typology, as well as the fundamental provisionality and inexactitude of an exercise which is designed primarily to be useful rather than 'true'.

This analysis has already begun to leak into the realm of manner or style, or the *how* of theology, which will be the governing concern of the next category, Etiquette theology. Meanwhile, what can be seen from this Worldview categorization is that the worldview in each case will tend to suggest a stylistic or methodological range. Of course, these may overlap, and types may resonate with each other across the categories. For instance, a bias towards a view that focuses on the world and the human condition might favour indigenous human reason as its best sense-making tool, but so might a view that focuses on the transcendent God, albeit using different philosophical tools. Revelation might well be considered more important than reason for those favouring the 'between' focus, but reason might be considered to be revelation by the other two, or at least as a necessary tool for making sense of it. Regardless of style, each of the Worldview types has a particular concern with communicating something particular about belief. Not so our second cluster, which is more concerned with the 'how' than the 'what' of theology.

3

Etiquette Theology

The second cluster is called the Etiquette group, because each concerns theological method or approach. After Langdon Gilkey, David Kelsey would call this category as a whole 'theological methodology', or 'something a theologian does to solve a problem he faces in getting started at doing theology' (Kelsey 1975, p. 7). 'Style' might be another term, but Etiquette is concerned with normative social conventions and behaviour, and as such provides a useful frame for the governing preoccupation of this type of theology. In general, Etiquette typologists sort by 'discipline', often borrowing from the academic categories of the arts, sciences and social science. In contrast to the Worldview types, their governing preoccupation is not about versions of reality, but about how theological languages and disciplines relate to non-theological ones, particularly in the public arena. And perhaps it is predictable that modern theological discourse in a plural context should be characterized by a preoccupation with etiquette, because of a concern on the part of the believing theologian not to be duplicitous or dishonest.

David Tracy

Cheat sheet

Chicago's David Tracy wrote his seminal book *The Analogical Imagination* in 1981. He did so to argue that, of course, we can only understand the divine by analogy. In the book he introduces a typology that differentiates theology by audience. When we talk to the Church, we deploy Systematic theology. When we talk to the academy, we use Fundamental theology; and when we talk to society, we use Practical theology. In the first instance, our conversation concerns the Beautiful. For the academy, the True; and for society, the Good. And this means that the theologian is also in a different mode: the quality of their belief is important for their credibility with the Church and with society. However, for the academy, their independence needs to be assured, because reason rather than faith is the primary discourse. His typology is therefore usefully clear that the audience addressed affects the mode both of the theology and of the theologian involved.

In his 1981 book *The Analogical Imagination*, Tracy argues that, in the face of pluralism, a new theological strategy is required, to 'avoid privatism by articulating the genuine claims of religion to truth'. This strategy he calls the 'analogical imagination', because he holds that 'each of us understands each other through analogy or not at all' (Tracy 1981, pp. ix, 447, repeated on pp. 451ff., 452, 454). In service of articulating these religious claims to truth, Tracy notes the fundamentally public nature of theology and therefore identifies its three 'primary publics', namely society, the academy, and the Church. He contends that these publics call for three types of 'distinct but related' disciplines in theology, such that the academy is addressed through Fundamental theology, the Church through Systematic theology, and society through Practical theology (pp. 56ff.). While the three vary in approach, they share two 'constants', in that all theologies seek to interpret the religious tradition, and to interpret the religious dimension of the contemporary situation. These two constants deliver the criteria of *appropriateness* in terms of the religious tradition and *understandability* in terms of the contemporary situation (p. 91 n.66). This commonality provides the basis for shared discourse among theologians, about whether or not a given approach accurately analyses a given situation, and about whether or not a given situation has a religious dimension that requires a theological response. Specifically, the three approaches differ in their view of what constitutes a public claim to 'truth' in theology (pp. 61ff.).

First, Fundamental theology, which addresses itself primarily to the academy. In this mode, truth claims are adjudicated through philosophy or another established academic discipline. Established rules of argumentation are therefore used both to explain and to justify religious truth claims. Thus, 'the word "public" here refers to the articulation of fundamental questions and answers which any attentive, intelligent, reasonable and responsible person can understand and judge in keeping with the requirement for fully public criteria for argument'. Here reason is primary, and personal faith or beliefs are not 'warrants or backings' for publicly defended claims to truth. Tracy identifies Augustine, Aquinas and the Scholastics as particular exemplars of this theological tradition (pp. 62–4).

Second, Systematic theology, which addresses itself primarily to the Church. For Tracy, the Systematic theologian's major task is the reinterpretation of the tradition for the present situation. In order to guard against idolatry, and to provide a vantage point from which to make its universal truth claims, theology in this mode is unashamedly and distinctively Christian, and does not hesitate 'to begin with its own inner history and reflect upon its own special occasion or illuminating event as the properly self-evidencing reality of its real foundation'. Because this mode requires 'constant mutually critical correlations' between the classical tradition and contemporary experience, the Systematic theologian has a public role as the hermeneutical expert in a particular genre of the cultural classics, reinterpreting their 'truth' age by age. Tracy regards H. Richard Niebuhr's book *The Meaning of Revelation* as an exemplar of this theological type (Tracy, pp. 64–8).

Tracy's third type is Practical theology, which addresses itself primarily to society. This mode regards truth as 'authentic subjectivity', tested by 'whether one speaks the truth by doing the truth'. Theology cannot therefore be divorced from the praxis of the theologian, who must evidence some form of authentic personal involvement and/or commitment. Thus, Practical theology is characterized by concern with 'concrete intellectual, moral and religious praxis of concrete human beings in distinct societal and historical situations'. Its tools are therefore unapologetically historical and socio-scientific in order to ensure the accuracy of its diagnosis, in that in this mode 'praxis is theory's own originating and self-correcting foundation'. Political and liberation theologies are representative of theology of this type. Tracy notes that one particular virtue of this sort of theology is that in shifting the focus from theory to praxis it shifts attention away from the preoccupations of the Christian intellectual over a crisis of cognitive claims towards the 'social-ethical crisis of massive suffering and widespread oppression and alienation in an emerging global culture'. In noting this virtue, he warns of its corresponding vice, lest praxis become 'fact fetishism' or uncritically mediated practice, or criticism be dismissed as infected by 'foreign' ideologies or *ad hominem* condemnation of the relevant theologian (pp. 69–78).

Tracy notes that the types are distinctive in five regards: their 'public', their mode of argument, their emphasis in ethical stance, their self-understandings of the theologian's personal faith or beliefs, and their formulation of what primarily counts as meaning and truth in theology. He uses 'Aristotelian' keywords to convey the essence of the activity; and the device of the true, the beautiful and the good to explain their focus with regard to the religious or holy (pp. 56–8, 85 n.31). These differences can be tabulated thus:

	Fundamental	Systematic	Practical
Type of public	Academy	Church	Society
Mode of argument	Public discourse via formal reason	Tradition-telling and re-telling	Praxis drives theory not vice versa
Ethical stance	Loyalty to academic standards of enquiry	Loyalty to the religious tradition	Solidarity with specific practitioners
The theologian	Independent	Committed believer	Committed believer
Meaning and truth	Academically accepted categories	Hermeneuticians of accepted truths	Praxis-based, prophetic and transfor-mative
Key concepts	Dialectic, metaphysics	Rhetoric, poetics	Politics, ethics
Focus	The True	The Beautiful	The Good

While his typology is treated here first for chronological reasons, it is a particularly robustly argued and influential one. It usefully highlights the 'public' or audience as a key variable in determining theological mode, and identifies the two 'constants' which in his view underlie all theology: the interpretation of the religious tradition, and the interpretation of the religious dimension of the contemporary situation. A further variable he introduces is that of the faith position of the theologian, not only in terms of the truth claims being made, but also in terms of the credibility of the theologian as a messenger for those claims. It also flags the notion of warrants and backings, which is a salutary reminder to anyone addressing the public square. After Toulmin, a warrant is a general hypothetical statement that answers the question 'how did you get there?' asked in response to data produced in support of a claim or conclusion. A backing lends authority to a warrant, and is likely to be field-dependent, that is, specific to the argument in hand. While a backing may be as categorical a statement of fact as the original data supplied in support of the contention and in response to the trigger question 'what have you got to go on?', its function in the argument is what distinguishes it (Toulmin 2003, pp. 89ff.). Where ontology differs, the underlying worldview needs to be transparent.

One gap in Tracy's typology would appear to be a type lying somewhere between the Fundamental and Practical types. It would still have 'society' as its audience, but it is a theology that is more apologetic than exhortatory in style. Neither does it adhere to quite the rigour or protocol demanded by the academy, in that it is the mode of theology that seeks to explain (or interpret) the religious tradition and the religious dimension of the contemporary situation in the indicative but not the imperative mood. In this way it could be considered a sub-type of either of these two Tracy parents, having a different flavour depending on the faith position of the theologian involved. One way to tease out this nuance is to recall the typology employed by James Gustafson, in identifying four varieties of moral discourse: prophetic, narrative, policy and ethical. 'Prophetic' discourse tends to condemn current failures and exhort believers to realize a utopian vision. 'Narrative' discourse uses stories to sustain traditions. 'Policy' discourse is a pragmatic mode seeking to identify possible ways forward in a pluralistic social setting; while 'ethical' discourse involves rigorous moral argumentation, self-critical reflection, and intellectual respect for diverse points of view (Gustafson 1988, pp. 268ff.). In this analysis, there is a differences of intent that determines the differences in genre and methodology. Thus, while Tracy's Fundamental theology is likely to make most use of ethical discourse, his Systematic, narrative, and his Practical, prophetic, there may be a further style of 'apologetic' theology that is akin to Gustafson's policy discourse. While this further style might not be quite as sophisticated as evidence to a Parliamentary Select Committee, it is at least adapted to make it accessible to the proverbial reader of *The Sun* newspaper. Contemporary examples of this mode are to be found in the variety of theological responses that have been offered to the public in the wake of the huge popularity of books by Dan Brown, Philip Pullman and Richard Dawkins. More generally, a segmentation of Tracy's publics – elevating his typology to a taxonomy – would serve as a useful test of his primary categories.

As well as the apologetic or exhortatory intent or segmentation that suggests the subdivision of the Fundamental and Practical types, his Systematic mode could also be subdivided. In this case, the Church already has a convenient subdivision that could be used, which brings to the surface a key elision in Tracy's typology. While orthodoxy may well correspond with orthopraxy, they are different categories, and as above would be deployed differently in the indicative and imperative moods. A broadening of this category to include these emphases and moods shades in to Tracy's Practical type, but is still firmly addressed to the Church and not to society at large.

The distinction Tracy makes between the Fundamental and Systematic is also problematic, in terms of the faith position of the theologian. In Fundamental theology, Tracy holds them to be independent, which renders the Systematic subordinate to the Fundamental as regards 'the true'. This would appear to assume the primacy of reason in the court of theological law, and does not accommodate disagreement within the Church between believers. This position is a defensible one but does suggest an implicit hierarchy or ordering of the types which Tracy does not explicitly own, whereby the Fundamental acts as the 'licence to operate' for the other two. It also assumes a mode of reasoning where faith can be 'shelved' for the purposes of clean public argument, another assumption that would appear to require justification.

George Lindbeck

Cheat sheet

Yale's George Lindbeck was, with Hans Frei, one of the founding fathers of the post-liberal movement. Frustrated by the constriction of the labels 'conservative' and 'liberal' he set about creating a more precise description of what theology does. His 1984 typology hyphenates lots of words in order to improve the quality of ecumenical dialogue, and wins the prize for jargon. Broadly, his cognitive-propositional type is religion as philosophy; his experiential-expressive is religion as aesthetic phenomenon; and his cultural-linguistic is religion as one of Wittgenstein's language games. His clever manoeuvre therefore is to use the permission granted by the 'language game' terminology as a Trojan horse to smuggle the other two into public discourse.

In 1984, Lindbeck set out his three approaches to theology in order that he might contextualize and promote the third in particular, in the service of more effective ecumenical dialogue. He posits three comparators: propositional truth, symbolic efficacy and categorical adequacy, and renders each as a distinct type: the cognitive-propositional, the experiential-expressive and the cultural-linguistic (Lindbeck 1984, p. 47).

The first type, the cognitive-propositional, emphasizes the cognitive aspects of religion, stressing 'the ways in which church doctrines function as informative propositions or truth claims about objective realities'. In this mode, religion behaves as a philosophy or a science, and represents the traditional orthodox or 'fundamentalist' approach. This type is somewhat similar to Tracy's Fundamental academic type, except that for Tracy the theologian would appear to need to be seen to be more independent in this mode than for Lindbeck. Popular champions of this type in the last century for Lindbeck would be G. K. Chesterton,

C. S. Lewis and Malcolm Muggeridge, although in his view the type has now been challenged by history and by science – and by the 'deobjectification' of religion and doctrine – and has lost ground to the second type (pp. 16, 20ff.).

This second type, the experiential-expressive mode, interprets doctrines as 'noninformative and nondiscursive symbols of inner feelings, attitudes, or existential orientations'. In this mode, religion behaves like an aesthetic enterprise, and religions are seen as 'multiple suppliers of different forms of a single commodity needed for transcendent self-expression and self-realization'. Religions become possible sources of symbols 'to be used eclectically in articulating, clarifying, and organizing the experiences of the inner self', and the type is future-proofed by its feeling of perpetual 'relevance'. Represented for him by Bernard Lonergan (and indeed Tracy), Lindbeck regards this type as being particularly congenial to liberal theologians, and notes that its ready marketability makes it attractive to theologians, ministers and teachers of religion. He does, however, query its ready acceptance of the universalizability of religious experience. This type is at the same time identical and opposite to Tracy's Systematic church type, depending on the viewpoint of the observer. Seen from without, Tracy's type would indeed be one experiential-expressive religious stall among many, while from within it, Lindbeck's type would appear too subjective and individualistic in feel to conform to Tracy's orthodoxy (pp. 16, 22, 25, 31ff., 38, 40–2).

Lindbeck's preferred type is the cultural-linguistic type, which emphasizes the resemblance of religions to languages and cultures, that is, as parallel idioms 'for the construing of reality and the living of life', or, in Wittgenstein's parlance, a 'language game'. If the experiential-expressive type privileges the formative nature of the inner world, the cultural-linguistic type reverses this to privilege the formative nature of the outer world, through language and culture. Church doctrines are thus used as 'communally authoritative rules of discourse, attitude, and action'. This is much closer to Tracy's understanding of his Systematic church type in terms of its internal integrity, although again, from the outside, it will appear to others less 'true' by comparison with other religious 'games' than it feels to an insider. Indeed, Lindbeck notes that a problem with this type, in comparison with the first two, is its fundamental relativity, in that the first two admit 'truth', even if the second type approaches it indirectly, and are more transcendental in their orientation. Additionally, the prosaic and worldly origins of languages and cultures make this type 'suspiciously secular-looking' (pp. 18, 30, 34).

For Lindbeck, his third type acts as an 'enlarged narrative' which can be used to harmonize the first two and to turn the horizontal logic of his typology into the vertical logic of a taxonomy. Thus, the cognitive-propositional becomes 'abiding doctrinal grammar' and the experiential-expressive 'variable theological language' within a cultural-linguistic language game called Religion. Additionally, he casts his typology in historical terms, rendering the three methodologically in sequence pre-liberal, liberal and post-liberal (pp. 112ff.). This sequencing allows him to speculate on their relative cultural attractiveness, where he awards the experiential-expressivist 'liberal' mode first place, given its ability to act as a unifying element in an individualistic but pluralist and divided world. However, he argues that the post-liberal cultural-linguistic mode has the most potential, in that it mirrors inter-disciplinary developments in preferring intratextual description to apology, making it best suited to dialogue in a post-Christian world. In commending the cultural-linguistic approach, he notes that 'those who think that religions are more the sources than the products of experience will regard a loss of religious particularity as impoverishing, while others will consider it enriching'. Although it may look 'secular' and relativist, he argues that of the three it is best placed to honour the position that religious utterances only become 'real' ontologically when their correspondence is established through 'performance', in the playing out of the language game which unites cognitive-propositional objectivity with experiential-expressivist subjectivity (pp. 65ff., 126–30). This distinction in theology between potentiality and actuality will be revisited later on in this chapter.

Lindbeck's typology is compelling. It acts as a typology, a topology and taxonomy all at once, and its pragmatic focus renders it particularly suitable for the ecumenical goal he has in mind. Lindbeck serves to contribute the key variable of stance to this exercise, in that, when compared with Tracy, the respective positions of the theologian and the 'public' being addressed in each case becomes important as a way of understanding how their typologies vary. While his neat mapping of the three types across a temporal spectrum is perhaps less persuasive, it does serve to identify the importance of the intellectual context in which the theologian is operating, which is again an important point of etiquette to facilitate the involvement of theology in inter-disciplinary dialogue. He also considers the notion of 'attractiveness' which is a step towards the segmentation of 'publics' suggested above, the better to hone the tools of theological communication to greatest effect.

Unhelpfully, Lindbeck's categories make an ontological assumption which may limit their purchase. In his taxonomy, the cultural-linguistic language game called Religion subdivides into the cognitive-propositional 'abiding doctrinal grammar' and the experiential-expressive 'variable theological language'. This commits the relativism he abhors in the liberal approach, rendering the construct a container of truth as opposed to the communication of an 'external' absolute of some kind. His self-critique admits this, dismissing it with a version of the argument that the proof of the pudding is in the eating, but his resulting position is (knowingly) weakened thereby. It strengthens the apologetic competence of theology at the expense of its exhortatory potential. Lindbeck does not therefore have a type that corresponds to Tracy's Practical societal type except in its indicative mood.

Generally, Lindbeck's typology works best as a taxonomy, tactically because it smuggles into any dialogue the other two types by default, and logically because the difference between his experiential-expressive and cultural-linguistic types is not otherwise wholly convincing. His logic rests on an inner/outer world distinction which introduces as variables the subjective/objective category without applying these to his cognitive-propositional type which privileges objectivity. This brings to the surface an epistemological assumption about the cognitive-propositional type which again may not stand scrutiny if, as he intends through dialogue, theology in that mode is subject to critique through the lenses of other disciplines. This problem is however resolved by his conversion of the typology into a taxonomy, which neatly relativizes the objectivity of the cognitive-propositional approach.

Hans Frei

Cheat sheet

Hailing from the Yale stable and taught by Richard Niebuhr, Hans Frei draws a general distinction between 'top-down' and 'bottom-up' theology. Top-down theology starts from philosophical first principles, whereas bottom-up theology is rooted in the 'grammar' of the faithful. This is because of the necessary progression from one to the other. In First-Order theology, the theologian is exploring the creeds and worship of the faith community. In Second-Order theology, the theologian is scrutinizing these to uncover their implicit rules and logic. In Third-Order theology, the theologian is putting the discourse into context alongside other 'ruled discourses' in order to explain it to outsiders. Like the other Etiquette theologians, Frei is at pains to ensure that theologians do not confuse one mode with the other, lest they end up at cross-purposes and unable to be effective.

Edited after his death in 1988 and published in 1992, Frei's typology of modern Western Christian theology was to have provided a 'conceptual orientation' for a larger (unfinished) historical project about the figure of Jesus of Nazareth in England

and Germany since 1700. His concern in producing his typology was to avoid the oversimplification of the use of a spectrum (like radical to liberal) or the insufficiently encompassing use of a range of 'responses' (such as theological outlooks on science and culture). As a starting point, he identifies three aspects of Christian theology, which he calls First-, Second- and Third-Order theology. First-Order theology is essentially Christian witness, including the confession of specific creeds (a bit like Lindbeck's experiential-expressivist type and perhaps aspects of Tracy's Practical societal theology). This relates to, but is distinct from, Second-Order theology, which endeavours to bring out the rules implicit in First-Order statements (a bit like Tracy's Systematic church type, and overlapping slightly with Lindbeck's cognitive-propositional and cultural-linguistic types). The witnessing and the rules that inform it – the 'speech' and the 'grammar' – then become the subject of Third-Order theology, which seeks to place these in context, generally to explain to outsiders how they relate to other kinds of ruled discourse (a bit like Tracy's Fundamental academic type and related to Lindbeck's cognitive-propositional type) (Frei 1992, pp. 1, 20ff.).

This understanding of the three 'layers' of theology allows Frei to separate formal Western theology into two contrasting views or emphases: a top-down emphasis on 'philosophy' or a bottom-up emphasis on 'grammar'. He argues that these distinctions arise a priori from the fact that the truth claims of theology suggest theology is both praxis and theory. Since the knowledge it provides is deemed necessary for salvation, the relationship (if any) between 'the faith which is believed and the faith by which we believe' throws up this essential distinction between the objective and/or existential categories of theological language (p. 26). In drawing this distinction, he notes the inherent bias towards the objective 'philosophy' school, given that most theology is written by academics.

In the first 'philosophical' view, Christian theology is viewed as an instance of a general class or generic type, and can therefore be subsumed under general criteria of intelligibility, coherence and truth, alongside other academic disciplines, to which it submits. This pure type corresponds with Tracy's Fundamental academic type. In the second 'grammatical' view, theology is an aspect of Christianity and is therefore 'partly or wholly defined by its relation to the cultural or semiotic system that constitutes that religion'. In this view, theology is religion-specific and is explained by Christianity rather than vice versa. Christian theology thus comprises the formal statements and proclamations of Christian practice and belief, and the Christian community's appraisal of its own language and actions against these formative statements within the norms of the Christian community. This type corresponds with Tracy's Systematic type. This split between philosophy and grammar also maps on to Lindbeck's division of his cultural-linguistic mode into the cognitive-propositional and experiential-expressivist sub-types (pp. 2, 19ff.).

Frei uses a range of relationships between philosophical and grammatical theology to generate five 'types' of theological method, which he illustrates in each case via a leading proponent. His first type he calls theology as a philosophical discipline, in which the academy takes priority over Christian self-description, and philosophy is the foundational discipline. In this type, exemplified for him by Gordon Kaufman's *Essay on Theological Method*, the task of the theologian – as metaphysician – is to search out the rules governing the use of the word 'God' as the organizing focus for a whole vocabulary. This renders Christian self-description subordinate to the larger metaphysical project, in that its 'sectarian' self-understanding is accountable to external description, arising from the general enquiry into ultimate meaning (pp. 28ff.).

In his second type, theology is still a philosophical or academic discipline, and philosophy is still primary, but it takes the specificity of Christianity more seriously, fusing the external description with the internal description into one foundational philosophical scheme. Frei suggests Tracy's *Blessed Rage for Order* as an exemplar of this type, in so far as he defines theology as philosophical reflection on human experience and the Christian tradition.

In this type, Christian 'fact' is correlated with common human experience, as two autonomous sources of theological reflection, to determine mutual compatibility (Frei 1992, p. 30).

Type three regards theology as an academic enterprise and as Christian self-description as equal, in that they must correlate, and neither has primacy over the other. He regards Schleiermacher as an ambiguous proponent of this type, represented in his *Outline of Theology* and *The Christian Faith*. Even Schleiermacher does not fit neatly into this typology, because Frei sees him as arguing against the primacy of philosophy as the overarching discipline of the previous two types, viewing it primarily as a useful quarry for definitions, criteria and language. Thus in Schleiermacher's version of this type, academic theology itself needs to correlate with philosophy (and other academic disciplines), and in turn with Christian self-description, as well as with external descriptions of Christianity as a phenomenon (Frei 1992, pp. 34ff.).

Frei's fourth type holds Christian self-reflection as having priority over academic theology. Using Barth, he illustrates this type through the introduction to *Church Dogmatics*, where Barth states that theology is a function of the Church because the Church is accountable to God for its discourse about God. However, while self-reflection is primary, philosophy still has a place, as a servant to theology in furnishing it with a 'draw-down' vocabulary, more as an ad hoc translator than as a systematic explicator. Within theology as self-description, Barth holds the *what* to be primary to the *how*, in that the logic or grammar of the faith is itself primary to how that faith is expressed in Christian living. In this way, the internal 'philosophy' of Christianity (its formal theology) is primary to its lived-out self-expression (Frei 1992, pp. 39–43).

This use of philosophy, either externally or internally, is banished by the fifth type, here epitomized for Frei by D. Z. Phillips. For him, meaning cannot be grasped apart from context – to ask a question about the reality of God is to ask a question about a kind of reality that can only be accessed from within the context of that reality: theology as 'inside talk'. Within this inside talk, authoritative statements or systems act as maps of the territory or keys to unlock internal meaning, but they have no meaningful external reference. He therefore rejects what he sees as the preju-dicial philosophical craving for generality, although he admits philosophy's usefulness in clarifying the complete distinctiveness of religion (Frei 1992, pp. 48–51).

Frei's typology is extremely useful, not least because of its starting point in returning to first principles, based on how theol-ogy behaves, using the layers of First-, Second- and Third-Order theology to derive his top-down/bottom-up dichotomy. Like Lindbeck, he offers a typology and a taxonomy, and contributes to a consideration of type the important notion of the end to which a given theology is being deployed. While this consider-ation was subsumed into the logic of the other typologies, Frei's 'layers' lend it greater clarity here. Ironically, although he warns against the easy simplicity of a spectrum like 'radical' and 'lib-eral', one of his most helpful contributions is his philosophy/grammar continuum, along which his five types range. In addi-tion, he usefully warns against opportunistic approaches to the-ology that produce a range of 'responses' to presenting issues, but that are not 'sufficiently encompassing' or convincingly logi-cal in their construction (p. 1).

A further contribution arises from Frei's harmonization across the divide by way of his definition of theological think-ing as 'a conceptual skill governed by practical aims'. This definition strikes at the heart of Frei's dilemma about theol-ogy as theory and/or praxis: is theology when described by one who inhabits its worldview (the theologian) different from theology when described by an onlooker (the social scientist)? Thus he echoes the relevance of Tracy's variable of the theolo-gian's belief (in addition to their intellectual context), in that where the theologian might see faith, the philosopher sees only metaphysics, the psychologist the transpersonal, and the social scientist, cultural anthropology or the sociology of religion (pp. 114, 129ff.).

Rowan Williams

Cheat sheet

Rowan Williams, formerly Archbishop of Canterbury, devised his 3Cs model to describe the varying register of his writings. Typically of his pithy prose, his is the briefest of the typologies explored, but covers similar ground to Tracy, albeit more efficiently. His types are the Celebratory, for Church talk; the Critical, for academic talk; and the Communicative, for public square talk. If you seek a simple but deep framework, his would be the one to borrow to describe most modes of theology. It also acts as a job description for the clergy, and particularly for bishops and archbishops, who need to be equally convincing in all three modes.

In the Prologue to his 2000 book *On Christian Theology*, Williams set out his 'typology of theological voices', in part to explain why the 'register' of some of his chapters might appear 'unstable', given his various public and academic roles. Loosely based on Schleiermacher's typology of preaching in *The Christian Faith* (the poetic, the rhetorical and the 'descriptively didactic' or scientific), he intended it to clarify the *interaction* between the types, as well as their status as provisional tools which, when used together, facilitate 'the delivery of believing utterances' in an arena where the 'methodology' can never be wholly clear. His is again a three-fold typology, of theology as Celebratory, Communicative and Critical, largely influenced after Tracy by the 'public' to whom it is addressed. Using the analogy offered by Mike Higton (Higton 2004a, pp. 10ff.), Williams' Celebratory mode is like using the mother-tongue in the home. His Communicative mode is like using a second language to enable international communication, while his Critical voice steps back to examine the grammar and the functioning of language itself to ensure that it is in good repair for the task in hand (Williams 2000a, pp. xvi, xiii–xvi and throughout).

Williams describes his Celebratory 'voice' as the rich and self-referential 'jargon', familiar in hymnody and preaching, which is most often used to communicate truths with a 'public' of fellow believers. As such, it can appear unintelligible to outsiders, but is 'an attempt to draw out and display connections of thought and image so as to exhibit the fullest possible range of significance in the language used'. This voice is similar to what Frei calls 'First-Order theology'. In his second mode, the Communicative voice, theology can be seen explaining, persuading or commending its truths to others using rhetoric borrowed from 'uncommitted environments' in order to address an uninitiated 'public'. Examples would be the use of Aristotle and Plato, Marx, or other 'indigenous' intellectual idioms in order to be better understood abroad. Equally, such colonizing of 'foreign' constructs can be used to shed further light on the theology in question. This voice is like Frei's Third-Order or philosophical theology, albeit with a communicative rather than a primarily self-reflective bent. It is reminiscent of a mixture of Tracy's Fundamental and Practical types, and akin to the act of deploying Lindbeck's cultural-linguistic taxonomy. His third voice, the Critical, involves theology 'nagging at fundamental meanings . . . alert to its own inner tensions or irresolutions', unselfconsciously questioning the very constructs of the Celebratory and Communicative modes. This type naturally tests and/or renews the other two, particularly in the face of novelty or innovation, and is most commonly encountered as 'philosophical theology'. This mode is like Frei's Second-Order theology, when it is not only explicating but challenging the grammar of the First Order, and like Tracy's Fundamental mode when it is ranging over his Systematic and Practical types in order to check their health. It is also a version of Lindbeck's cognitive-propositional type, again where it interfaces with the content of his other two. Unlike these types, it does not cede to philosophy or other 'external' disciplines for defence or criticism, but uses them as critical friends to test the integrity of theology on its own terms (2000a, pp. xiii, xiv, xv; Higton 2004a, p. 14).

In identifying his typology, Williams is at pains to describe it as an exercise in 'displaying modes of arguing and interpretation' rather than the advancing of a single system. While typically sparse and understated, he encapsulates in a few pages what it takes Tracy, Lindbeck and Frei a book apiece to accomplish. This deceptively simple typology usefully points up the key variables identified above: the public being addressed, the faith context, the relative stances of the parties, and the end to which the theology is being deployed. Where it does not reach Frei is in explicitly flagging the intellectual context, or Tracy in defining a mode that would take his Communicative voice beyond explication, by employing some of the flavour of the Celebratory to influence and persuade. He offers his typology to explain the interaction between the types as well as their different flavours, and he does this by suggesting that the three operate in an essentially 'restless' relay, with each taking a turn when the preceding type gets tired. Honouring this team dynamic, he warns that to form them into a hierarchy would be to misunderstand the way theology works (2000a, p. xvi).

Beyond the elegance of the model, the introduction of the notion of the 'Celebratory' usefully captures the more 'active' feel of this type of 'first-order' theology and, like Lindbeck's experiential-expressivist mode, is in contrast to the passivity of Tracy's Systematic type or Frei's grammar. His metaphorical distinction between speaking a language and maintaining it is also an efficient way to encapsulate much of the intent of Tracy's Fundamental, Lindbeck's cognitive-propositional and Frei's philosophical theology, although these vary slightly among themselves, often shading into Williams' Communicative mode in their intention.

Because the occasion of his typology is to make sense of his own writings, the underlying logic or guarantee about its deployment is in this case himself, so his typology is silent on whether and how the faith of the theologian affects the theology deployed. Admittedly, Williams is clear that his categories do not represent 'an advance towards an ideal form of fully self-conscious reflection', but clarity on this point would be particularly helpful in understanding the transition between the Communicative and the Critical modes. The distinction between them, expressed by Tracy as the independence of his Fundamental theologian, lies at the heart of much of the current debate about public theology. Whether or not theology is fixing itself from within or without returns the discussion to the core debate about the fundamental relationship between theology and philosophy, and the status of theological language (2000a, p. xiii).

Etiquette Synthesis

While Tracy's is arguably the most developed of the Etiquette typologies, the others contribute a range of illuminating facets to add colour to this cluster. Some use the categories of academia to determine method (Hans Frei), some talk about the different 'languages' of believers and those who hold different world-views (George Lindbeck), and some try to describe the mood of the different theological approaches that are used (Rowan Williams). Taken as a whole, they suggest a number of variables that should be considered in Etiquette theology. First, the public being addressed will affect the theological mode. Whether or not the audience is part of the theological tradition will also affect register, as will the beliefs and the intellectual context of the theologian. Whether the parties believe in subjective or objective truths will also have a bearing on the theological discussion, and the purpose of the discussion will affect the mood of the theology deployed and whether it is in the active or the passive voice. As Lindbeck puts it, the aim of concepts is to remove anomalies, so the delineation between types, the etiquette of their deployment, and their inter-relationship must also be clear.

A bit like a scatter graph, these variables appear to home in on a few fundamental areas. This allows them to be described in a simple framework, because the style of theology employed adjusts according to audience and scope. One contextual distinction is between theology that is concerned with thought or belief, and theology that is concerned with being or action. For convenience these might be termed *doxy* and *praxy*. This division honours the variable of intention, where the purpose of a given theology affects both style and content.

The use of doxy and praxy in this context merits further explanation. Aristotle's classic notion of potentiality and actuality is useful here (Kenny 1998, pp. 74–8). Using the example of language, Aristotle argues that there is a difference between not knowing Greek, knowing Greek, and speaking Greek. In the first instance the person involved is in a state of sheer potentiality. When they first learn Greek, they enter the stage of 'first actuality', in that they have realized their potential to learn the language. This first actuality, though, still constitutes a state of potentiality unless the person decides to exercise their 'rational powers' and decide to enter the 'second actuality' of speaking Greek. This property of potentiality is therefore a person's capability to undergo change. Thus, a split between doxy and praxy suggests the transition between potentiality and actuality; between knowing theology and performing theology in everyday life.

A second distinction adds the variable of mood. Mood has already been mentioned as a variable in type, and it is a particularly useful lens for examining the 'Etiquette' category. David Ford's book *Christian Wisdom* opens with a confession about his having been surprised by the 'cries' in that research. In examining these cries, he explores their moods: indicative, imperative, interrogative, subjunctive and optative (Ford 2007, pp. 4f.). More generally than Ford's five, in linguistics, mood is split into two groups, *realis* and *irrealis*. Realis moods relate to things that are the case, for instance, things expressed in the indicative mood. Irrealis moods relate to things that are not the case, either because they will never be the case, or because they are not yet the case, for instance, things expressed in the subjunctive mood (Palmer 2001, pp. 1ff., 145ff.).

Most theology favours the indicative mood, although the imperative is also frequently deployed, and the interrogative features in some 'philosophical' theology. In the typologies considered, the indicative mood is the most commonly employed.

The imperative creeps in to Tracy's Practical societal type, and would undoubtedly be employed in Williams' Celebratory mode. The interrogative is also likely to feature prominently in the critical 'philosophical' theologies identified. But, given the variety of worldviews at play in the audiences involved, the less well-known notion of irrealis moods is a particularly useful one. In an 'irrealis' type there would be conditionality, either because the audience did not share the same faith, or because the 'backing' of faith was being – at least nominally – suspended for the purposes of philosophical scrutiny. Of course, irrealis types could also be used to exhort (as opposed to dictate) changes in behaviour, whether among the faithful or more generally, but in all irrealis cases the theological style would be designed to persuade not just to inform.

This sort of segmentation produces a grid that looks like this, with the above types mapped against it:

	Realis	Irrealis
Doxy	Systematic Celebratory Cognitive-propositional Grammar	Fundamental Critical Cultural-linguistic Philosophy
Praxy	Practical Celebratory Experiential-expressive	Practical Communicative

Arranged together, the doxy/praxy and realis/irrealis distinctions usefully suggest possibility, by introducing the visual idea of crossing the lines between the categories. One possibility is the use of theology to encourage a change from knowing to doing or from doing to knowing: the doxy/praxy frontier. Another is the use of theology to convert irrealis to realis by word or deed; or the conversion of realis to irrealis in order to persuade.

However, in order to accommodate the full range of Etiquette variables identified, this segmentation requires an accompanying rule of use. While it accommodates the notions of publics, belief and purpose, the segmentation does not yet help to define the terms of theological interaction. This is because it assumes all theologians are chameleons, and it assumes too much homogeneity within the irrealis mode. To mobilize this segmentation, the theologian first needs to establish the parameters of the interaction by deciding which 'squares' are involved in the dialogue. If the dialogue crosses the categories of realis and irrealis, particular care needs to be taken in order to ensure that the message is correctly communicated. This is because the divide crosses an ontological boundary and introduces a level of uncertainty that does not pertain within the realis sphere, and vice versa. For example, the realis/irrealis boundary is the one where a number of the theologians examined switch to a 'secular' language like philosophy or ethics in order to be better heard, particularly when their audience does not share their faith. If the dialogue crosses the categories of doxy and praxy, the person of the messenger becomes primary, as a warrant for the authenticity of the message. In this instance, the theologian will need to establish their credentials more formally – using an epistemology favoured by the target audience – before delivering their message, to ensure it appears credible.

This framework already shows promise for engagement with public theology and consumerism, because it is primed to cope with the secular through the device of the irrealis moods. But it is not yet the complete picture. And if an attempt was made to populate this grid with all known theologies, there is likely to be a bias towards theologies that focus on right thinking (potentiality) rather than right doing (actuality), although Williams' Celebratory category spans both. Arguably, Frei's notion of 'grammar' could also relate to praxy, mirroring the Celebratory category directly. Of course, this is likely to be an occupational hazard of a focus by academics on method. But for many people, the desire to engage theologically with public discourses like economics is often precipitated by bad behaviour, not bad thoughts, which tend to be less public. So how can both Worldview and Etiquette theology be used to do good theology in this space?

4

Good Theology

This book promotes a particular theological take on consumerism. In order for the reader to be able to assess its message, we need to establish what the hallmarks of a good theology of consumerism might be. What kind of criteria should such a theology meet? I have started to answer this question by explaining that all theology seems to fall into one of two categories: the Worldview category, or the Etiquette category. If it belongs to the former, its essential preoccupation will either be about God, the world or what lies between them. This includes theologies of churchmanship, sector and trend; hermeneutical categories like feminist and liberation theologies; and distinctions between denominations, traditions and geographies. If theology hails from the Etiquette camp, its essential preoccupation will be about how to 'do' theology, in a variety of different contexts. Theologies of process, style, method and philosophy all fit here. In the context of engagement with consumerism, a good theology would be alive to all of these nuances, to avoid a charge of bias or partiality. Perhaps a theology could be good *and* partial, as long as it was overtly so, but the stakes are high in this area of engagement, and a partial theology can be too readily dismissed. Most importantly, good public theology needs to pay proper attention to the central dilemma of theologies of Etiquette: regardless of the sophistication of the approach utilized, how do you speak respectfully and with integrity to those who do not share your worldview? Particularly, how do you do so if, as a theologian, your intention in using Etiquette is to earn the right to talk Worldview?

The beginning of a taxonomy of typologies has already been established through the identification of these two poles, of Worldview theologies and theologies of Etiquette. However, a prior logical split concerns an assumption embedded in the Worldview cluster, of shared belief in God. In the Etiquette cluster, this assumption is made in the person of the theologian, and asymmetrical belief is catered for in a number of the theological approaches specified. Using Frei's terminology, this is likely a result of a natural 'reversal'. Shared belief allows Frei's First-Order theology to be primary, with Second- and Third-Order theology likely to be of more passing or academic interest, for example, periodic discussion over the place of women in the Church. However, where belief in God is not shared, the assumptions that support First-Order theology cannot be gainsaid, rendering necessary a re-visitation of Third-Order issues to establish the credibility of Second- and First-Order issues in turn. Looked at through the other end of the telescope, it is predictable that modern theological discourse in a plural context should be characterized by a preoccupation with etiquette, because of the need to negotiate the terms of engagement in a contested ontological space.

The debate begun in Tracy about the necessarily public nature of theology runs on. All theology is 'words about God', so there is a third-person flavour to the discourse, lending it an objective slant that invites scrutiny. And while the person of the theologian has already been discussed and as a critical variable, the variable that arguably shapes discourse most is its intended audience or target – Tracy's 'publics'. Above his threefold split into the academy, the Church, and society, is the fundamental differentiation within these audiences between shared belief and asymmetrical belief. Given the working assumption that theology is *directed* in some way, this split provides the overarching taxonomic logic, not least because it dictates the kinds of warrants and backings that are likely to characterize the discourse thereafter.

This logic suggests a primary taxonomic split about belief, and a secondary split concerning Worldview/Etiquette. For simplicity, the belief axis will be labelled church (fellow believers) and world (those who do not share the Christian worldview), on the basis that while there is no homogeneity of belief in either camp, those in the non-church category cannot be assumed to respect the same warrants and backings that are currency within the Church.

By way of illustration, the specimen typologies can be grouped according to this logic, first whether belief is shared between theologian and audience, then by Worldview/Etiquette type. For example, the typologies of Cobb, Kort and Jones, and Niebuhr's Christ and Culture type, would cluster under the Church/ Worldview umbrella, joined there by hermeneutical or sector theologies, churchmanship or denominational theologies, theological movements such as Radical Orthodoxy, and any other theologies that address the substance of a believer's belief. In this context, a theology directed at existing members of the Church of England designed to articulate orthodox thinking on consumerism would reside in this theological family. An example of this kind of thing might be the chapter on money in the Doctrine Commission's 2003 report *Being Human*.

Next are the theologies that address fellow believers in the churches, but concern the etiquette or style of the theology rather than its content, such as Lindbeck's experiential-expressive or cognitive-propositional types, Williams' Celebratory or Critical types, Tracy's Systematic type and Frei's grammar type. Other theologies fitting this categorization would be theology as drama and Ford on mood, or any other theology that concerns the *how* rather than the *what* of theology, conducted within the community of shared Christian belief. In discussion about economics and consumerism, any theology that sets out a methodology for engaging with the subject belongs to this family, e.g. middle axioms being designed for church use, albeit with one eye on exterior credibility.

Any public theology that focuses on the rules of engagement in asymmetric belief contexts belongs in the third family grouping. The types of theology represented here, addressed to those in the world who do not share a belief in God – generally the academy or society – are most commonly concerned with etiquette and procedure, as has already been noted. Lindbeck's cultural-linguistic, Tracy's Fundamental and Frei's philosophy types primarily address the academy. Williams' Communicative type addresses society, although one could argue that it is designed for apology, and so straddles the Etiquette and Worldview categories here.

Theologies in an asymmetrical belief context that privilege 'content' are only here represented by Tracy's Practical type. More generally, it appears that Worldview types that assume shared belief are redeployed into asymmetric belief contexts when the need arises, appropriately rendered to appear palatable, and primarily with apologetic intent. Although Tracy's Practical mode is designed to function both apologetically and dialectically, there is otherwise a gap in the dialectical area, which in this context would be a public theology that is interested in secular insight, challenge and correction. And it is a cornerstone of theology in this 'box' that it should be reflexive, as a matter of etiquette. After Tracy's Practical theology, perhaps the middle axiom approach might sidle into this sphere, where the use of 'secular' experts provides the necessary self-criticism. Better examples might be drawn from engagement with transpersonal psychology, the field of ethics, or the current popularity of the concept of happiness as an avenue of enquiry.

While this taxonomical device started primarily as a sorting exercise, it has served to identify a gap in public theology that would repay attention. A good example of where being set in an apologetic rather than a dialectic mode has been a missed opportunity would be the modern spirituality movement, particularly in a workplace setting. Largely held in suspicion by the Church and condemned by the academy for its apparent shallowness, the modern workplace is a growth area for spirituality (Roberts 2002, pp. 63, 74ff., 290ff.). Historically, Industrial Mission should have been on hand to foster this trend, because Industrial Mission was originally conceived as a project to uncover the work of God in steelworks and railway yards, to discover how God might be spoken of in the lives of largely unchurched working people. Over time, it has become a traditional apologetic sector ministry, complete with workplace chaplains who stand ready to absorb the overflow from overstretched HR and line-management welfare functions. The retreat of Industrial Mission from its original remit as a ground-up teasing out of latent theology – and a true exemplar of the Worldview/world type of theology – has created a vacuum others have been quick to fill with mindfulness and other quasi-religious spiritual substitutes, creating a new discipline that is firmly secular. This shuts theology out, making it ever harder for theologians to start conversations in a space that is now both conquered and colonized, but one into which the Church should have blazed the trail (Brown and Ballard 2006, p. 16; and Brown 2004, pp. 45ff.).

Assuming the faith of the theologian in question (without which the theology instead becomes sociology, anthropology, psychology, metaphysics or ethics), this type poses the question, what does theology look like in this space? It might also ask, how is God revealing himself to 'unbelievers' outside the influence of formal theology and the churches? It is likely, however, that the lack of obvious theologies here is a gap not of activity but of nomenclature and orthodox attention. A recent report by Theos, to mark its ten-year anniversary, provides a promising label for this general activity: social liturgy. In the report, Nick Spencer defines this as 'the practice of public commitment to the other that is explicitly rooted in and shaped by love of God'. Or, put simply, 'love of God in love of neighbour, worship as service' (Spencer 2016, pp. 50, 56). As this is a new and promising way to frame much Christian theological activity – or doxy-driven praxy – in the public square, it is worth examining the concept in more detail.

In writing *Doing Good*, Spencer is trying to make sense of a curious phenomenon: just as formal church attendance seems to be declining, Christian activity in terms of social outreach seems to be increasing. For instance, there are 15,000 more faith-based charities today than there were in 2006, with more new faith-based charities registering each year than secular ones. The report finds that the level of Christian social action is vast and growing: in England, over 10 million adults are now using the church for social services like mother and toddler groups, youth groups, foodbanks, community events, relationship support, financial education and

HOW TO DO THEOLOGY

access to the internet (Spencer 2016, p. 45). But what to call this effort, rooted as it is in the churches, but not confined to them?

It is 'social' because it is charitable public action; and Spencer opts for the word 'liturgy' because it captures the idea of generous service which could be directed towards the human other as well as towards the divine. It is recognizable to the outside world because it is marked by commitment and love, and the recognition that all social encounters are personal. This renders it distinct from more secular and transactional public services, which have become generic, bureaucratic and subject to the vicissitudes of transitory funding, so its hallmarks are 'persistence, relationality and localized engagement' (Spencer 2016, p. 50). And, because the view that everyone is in need of healing is fundamental to the Christian faith, Christian charity is theologically infused with solidarity. As Spencer puts it, it is not about those who are OK dispensing largesse to those who are not: 'theologically informed social liturgy becomes much more about the church's ability to welcome people into transformative relationships than simply addressing their needs or performing acts of charitable service' (Spencer 2016, p. 50).

In terms of the wider exercise, of seeking to identify theological activity that is both addressed to the world beyond the Church but that is also concrete rather than methodological, social liturgy seemingly fits the bill, because it is theology enacted. But it is not yet clear whether it can meet the other criterion identified for contested space, that it should remain deeply respectful of the worldview of the other by attending to mood. Without this nuance, activity in this box smacks of covert proselytism, if it appears indicative or imperative in style. Genuine engagement by theology in the public square needs also to be open to secular insight, challenge and correction: it needs to be demonstrably interrogative, subjunctive and optative, asking a version of Bonhoeffer's question, 'Who is Jesus Christ for us today?'

Spencer would argue strongly against any charge of proselytism: 'In the Sermon on the Mount, Christ is about as clear on the dynamics of gift and service as it is possible to be. Those who claim to follow him should not give with strings attached. Generosity should be generosity, not a covert exchange, whether for favours, social approval or converts' (Spencer 2016, p. 57). Further, he reminds all Christians of the message of 1 Peter 3.15, that they should at all times stand ready – if asked – to give an account for the hope that is in them. So perhaps in the context of 'fishers of men', the term bycatch is a useful one; those fish not targeted by the nets, but caught in them nevertheless. Spencer calls them 'supplementary goods', which are the commendable results but never the objective of social liturgy (Spencer 2016, p. 58).

The *Doing Good* report also points out that in any public discourse, where different people with different ideologies may often be talking past one another, concrete social action is now the closest thing there is to a *lingua franca* (Spencer 2016, pp. 64ff.). And the Church uses the information it gleans from this concrete social action – its social liturgy – to inform its public theology and to speak truth to power. Whether on the floor of General Synod or in the House of Lords, powerful stories are told about the daily realities of parish life, particularly in deprived areas of the country. Recently the Church has been able to ask particularly difficult questions about austerity and changes to welfare policy, because it operates the largest number of foodbanks in Britain, and so has first-hand experience of those driven to use them.

With the caveat that this last box of theology is therefore more of a window than a mirror, because of the necessity of deploying irrealis moods there in a spirit of reciprocity, it is now possible to draw a taxonomy of theological type, split by audience and type of theology. Such labelling would produce the following grid, with the flavour of each quadrant conjured up by these labels:

	Worldview	Etiquette
Church	**Preaching to the converted**	**Sharpening your pencil**
World	**Social liturgy**	**Clearing your throat**

My guess is that the level of comfort, theologically speaking, spirals clockwise from the top left. The discussion of faith with believers tends to be well resourced, through centuries of language, iconography, texts and liturgy. And thanks to its history, the Church has always taken seriously the need to brood over its behaviour, both within the Church and within the philosophical context of the day. But the classic goal of mission is to move people up from the bottom of the grid, through conversion, to the top. This makes it rather important not to rely solely on those theologies that already assume belief and therefore beg the question. All systems of thought, secular or otherwise, rely on beliefs of some kind, so the challenge for theology in this area is not relevance so much as intelligibility, and how receptive an audience is to hear them, hence the importance of modes such as Williams' Communicative one.

Looking at the grid as a whole, we can see that public theology is an exercise either in lining up the Church and priming it about how and what it might say and do, or about engaging with the world on the matter, via the equivalent of a pre-nuptial agreement. And perhaps we are so anxious to find our feet in the public square that we forget to spend time in all four of these squares, in order to be most effective in the one that might mean the most, sharing our worldview with a world that thinks it doesn't need it.

One thing that will tend to stymie the conversation before it has even started is bad manners, hence the vital importance of etiquette in this sphere. My rules for engagement are therefore a set of criteria, winnowed from this examination of theological type. They assess theology in terms of the extent to which it:

- knowingly addresses both shared and asymmetric belief contexts (church and world)
- articulates a worldview
- attends to methodological etiquette
- attends to Christian doctrine
- attends to Christian praxis
- flexes mood, with particular reference to audience and intent.

Arguably the most important criterion is the last one, because good public theology pivots around the issue of irrealis mood. This is because it immediately levels the playing field between the parties, by permitting questions, doubts, hopes and dreams. It adds to the necessary business of accounting for one's faith a mood of genuine inquiry.

Perhaps it is not often formally used because theologians are worried that forsaking realis constructions risks faithlessness or blasphemy. But, while tense conveys the time of an event, and aspect its nature, modality conveys the status of the *proposition* that describes the event, not the event itself. Technically, realis moods are used to portray situations that are actualized and thus knowable through direct perception, while irrealis moods portray situations that exist in the realm of thought and are thus known only through the imagination. But an utterance utilizing an irrealis mood need not mean that the event or topic *does not exist*, rather it denotes on the part of the speaker a studied diffidence. This distinction between statements of fact and statements of possibility – the difference between assertion and non-assertion – is a very helpful one in the context of a lack of shared worldview (Palmer 2001, pp. 1ff.; Palmer 1973, p. 83).

As a reminder, the under-utilized irrealis categories are the subjunctive, the optative and the interrogative, that is, speaking conditionally, expressing hopes and asking non-rhetorical questions. Perhaps Worldview theologies addressed to fellow believers could simply be redeployed, suitably adjusted for mood and language. But the Worldview/world section of the grid challenges the assumption inherent in the 'church' boxes that theology is primarily about 'telling', because etiquette in this instance demands listening as well as speaking. This sort of 'ontological listening' invites external challenge, and is a mode that Elaine Graham *et al.* have called the dialectical strand. In their usage, a distinction is made between apologetic witnessing, whether tempered for intelligibility or not, and the dialectical mode, in which theology stands open to secular insight, challenge and correction (Graham *et al.* 2005, p. 140). This suggests that, where theology is delivered into a world context, the theologies in question should indicate whether they are in 'transmit' or 'receive' mode by flexing mood. Thus, respectful public theology is likely to be attended by qualification, demonstrated through changes in mood, and characterized by a higher proportion of questions to statements.

Again, to be clear, this is not about the believer dissembling about their worldview or being duplicitous. As Jonathan Chaplin puts it, all those involved in public reasoning should be prepared for 'confessional candour' regarding the truth claims that lie behind their arguments. We all need to be able to articulate our warrants and backings. In a pluralist society, there can be no neutral ground, only mutual ground (Chaplin 2008, p. 70), and mood can be used to signal the openness that is a prerequisite for genuine dialogue.

In order to meet the criteria for engagement, this book pays attention to audience by addressing the Church in the first instance, while drawing on those parallel secular resources that might have currency in the public square. These additional resources, like empirically based studies drawn from social science, are provided throughout the following sections not to supplant or replace the theological resource, but to honour the fact that a non-Christian audience may not find the theology compelling and may need other arguments to bridge the gap. The Christian reader may not need them, but may find them useful in conversation with others. The book also sets out the worldview on which this analysis is based, namely a particular treatment of capitalism that suggests the need for urgent reform.

Methodologically, the book seeks to honour all of these criteria for theological health, and it draws on both Christian doctrine and Christian praxis to make the argument. As was noted above, mood is the particular innovation, which may feel unfamiliar to the reader, because it means that there are a lot of questions in this book. These are a deliberate attempt to provoke critical thought rather than a stylistic device, and have also been used to prime the resources at the end of the book. I hope they help.

This rather detailed look at theological theory has been an exercise in showing my workings. Public theology is too important and too disputed to assume that any given theologian will simply be taken on trust. So because the person of the theologian is also salient in this mode, I would conclude this long clearing of the throat by also inviting you to review the account of this theologian's credentials contained in the Preface. Now we are ready to address the matter in hand. Namely, what in the world is consumerism; what does God think about it; and what might we do about it as Christians?

PART TWO

God and Consumerism

5

What in the World is Consumerism?

We now have some idea about how theology behaves, and how it might be deployed to address consumerism. But what is consumerism, beyond the mere purchase of goods and services? Consumerism is a mode within capitalism that acts like an electric current within it. Consumerism switches capitalism on. If capitalism is the hardware, consumerism is the software that brings it to life. So before we return to a more formal consideration of consumerism, we need to look at its host, capitalism. And because capitalism has some design flaws, the survey will be a critical one.

Capitalism

Have you ever sold anything on eBay? eBay is a great way to explain market capitalism because it is such a pure version of the system. I want to pay for a holiday, so I sell off an old heirloom. Strangers compete with each other to buy it, checking out the going price by looking at similar transactions. We don't know each other, but eBay's feedback mechanism acts as a guarantee, because no one wants to deal with someone dodgy, so everyone tries hard to keep their ratings up. The system means that I get my holiday cash and the winner gets my heirloom. We're each acting selfishly in our own interests, but somehow everyone doing just that seems to work out over the longer term. If items don't appear on eBay very often, they attract a bidding war and high prices. If they are everyday items, they tend to follow a predictable pattern, with prices staying fairly stable over time. Looking at this more formally, there are seven big ideas that sit behind this kind of market.

First, the whole system assumes competition, on the grounds that it makes people try harder. This improves the quality of the market over time, as organizations vie with each other for market share, and people compete for jobs. Apple stays in the game by designing better products than its rivals. Supermarkets advertise price drops. And ambitious executives get an MBA to give them an edge in the job market. This is competition at work, improving the marketplace.

This welter of competitive activity is co-ordinated at the top by the so-called 'invisible hand'. This works imperceptibly, bringing together billions of customers and producers worldwide, matching supply to demand, such that everything works out right over all. What should be a chaotic mess somehow resolves into happy customers and rising profits, to the benefit of society as a whole.

And the biggest idea of all is that all we need to do to keep this process working is to be selfish. As Adam Smith put it, 'It is not from the benevolence of the butcher, the brewer, or the baker that we expect our dinner, but from their regard to their own self-interest' (Smith 1997, p. 119). Maximizing our own utility in any transaction we make leaves the invisible hand free to do its work. While we look out for ourselves, it resolves everything for us in the system as a whole.

The way the invisible hand does this is through pricing. The price of something acts as a signal to help match up people who want to buy things with the people who want to sell them. Low prices attract more customers, while high prices restrict demand to a smaller circle. So everyday items like toothpaste are cheap and readily available, while products that are rare, like Old Masters or vintage champagne, carry a high price. Changes in price affect buying behaviour, by making items more or less attractive. Provided governments let them be, markets use the ebb and flow of pricing to regulate supply and demand.

Within the system, people form organizations to generate wealth by producing goods and services. Most of them form companies, owned by shareholders who provided the money to set them up in the first place. These owners employ people as their agents, to work for them. But, because the market works best when we all pursue our own ends, there is a danger that the interests of the owners and their employees will diverge, as each seeks to maximize their own utility. This conflict of interest is called agency theory, and basically means that a lot of HR policy is about incentivizing employees to work in the interests of the owners.

Because the interests of the shareholders are so important, corporate strategy these days is all about how best to maximize shareholder value. This means keeping the share price high. Organizations use this barometer to set targets for staff. Many give their senior staff shares to make sure that the company's share price is always close to their heart.

And most of these companies are set up using the legal concept of 'limited liability'. This means that all the owners stand to lose if the company folds is the money they originally invested in it. This shields the owners from any downside, which encourages people to invest. This flow of new capital is the lifeblood of the market, and is vital to keep the wheels of the market perpetually turning.

So far, so good. But if you zoom in on any of these firm foundations, they start to blur and wobble. To make the system feel safe, the rules of the market tend to be positioned as fundamental laws of nature, which do not change over time. But even scientific truth is not this fixed. In science, temporary hypotheses have always been seen as the necessary roads to progress. A hypothesis generates a theory that is held until evidence emerges to disprove it. Not so for economists. Economics has become a victim of its attempt to look credible. It is so stuck in the past that it is now struggling to keep up with the facts as we see them today.

First, competition, the linchpin of the entire system. Rather than competition as a default, the mathematicians would argue in favour of cooperation as a primary strategy, because it yields better outcomes. While in war winning at all costs is necessary for survival, in business, companies want longer-term customer and supplier relationships. Those who treat transactions as battles to be won or lost sooner or later come a cropper, as their brand tarnishes and the market votes them out. On the other hand, cooperation and the sharing of information reduces wasteful duplication and increases the size of the pie, instead of restricting the debate to arguments about how best to cut it up. And competition is not just mathematically questionable, it is sexist, too. While male fight-or-flight physiology favours competition, particularly in challenging environments, it ignores the role that female physiology has to play. Research conducted on female subjects suggests a different and more mathematically useful physiological response, one that has been dubbed 'tend and befriend' (see Taylor *et al.* 2000). So being hooked on competition may actually be compounding a tendency towards suboptimal outcomes, reinforced through the norms of a traditionally masculine business environment.

Second, the invisible hand is just an optimistic myth. It offers a reassuring but inaccurate justification for self-interested behaviour. While order does frequently rise out of chaos, there is no evidence to suggest that this always tends towards the good, and certainly none sufficient to justify society's reliance on it. Birds flock into jet engines and fish shoal into the mouths of sharks. The crowd is sometimes wise, but not invariably so. In fact, leaving things to the invisible hand skews the market in favour of the strongest and most powerful, because their money means they have more 'votes' to cast into the marketplace. This maximizes their utility, but not that of society, or the world at large.

Third, the idea that 'utility' is the best way to measure the effectiveness and morality of the market only works if the invisible hand really exists. This is because the concept is an empty one – utility for what? And what happens if your utility is harmful to me? If there is no guarantee that individually selfish behaviours produce a good outcome overall, a system based on this thinking cannot be moral, without help. And the sort of help this requires – government intervention and the curtailment of freedoms – is exactly what the economists are trying to avoid, because it interferes with the smooth functioning of the market, and gets political, fast. Even if this idea was a sound one, the idea that Economic Man is a rational agent is wildly optimistic. We are all subject to irrational urges, whether through peer pressure, emotions or our psychological make-up. Assuming we are all robots just leads to confusion about how the market actually works, and about how best to run it.

Fourth, the assumption that the price mechanism, left to its own devices, will settle at a scientific equilibrium is nonsense. It ignores the interplay between supply and demand, and the potential for both of these to be manipulated. We see manipulation by cartels controlling the supply of assets like oil or diamonds; and parents particularly dread the pre-Christmas manipulation of children driven to a frenzy over the latest 'must have' piece of merchandized plastic. As well as air-brushing out the historical debate about 'just' prices and reasonable profit, market pricing ignores historical questions about cost. This obscures a very important debate about hidden costs, or 'externalities', like the social cost of drinking or smoking, or the cost of pollution. In an age where the limits of the planet are starting to be felt, it is vital that this debate about the market's embeddedness is not ignored. Cod disappeared from Newfoundland in 1992, and the planet is running out of other commodities all the time.

Fifth, agency theory. Adam Smith's original notion about the different interests of owners and managers has had catastrophic consequences. It has used negative psychology to generate HR policies that assume employee recalcitrance, limiting the ability of organizations to unlock human potential. Apart from the perhaps more justifiable practices of objective setting and timesheets, too many employers think it is entirely normal to apply a level of surveillance to their staff's every move that is an affront to human dignity. Worse, it's been used to justify the disastrous ubiquity of executive shareholding, in a move to force alignment. This practice, hand-in-hand with the idea of the supremacy of the shareholder, has made corporate strategy defiantly short-term and manipulative.

Sixth, the belief in the shareholder as king owes more to a romanticized ideal about the nature of shareholding than it does to reality. Ignoring the extremely limited legal sense in which shareholders actually 'own' businesses, modern patterns of share-holding and trading make the 'shareholder' a rather bizarre and certainly fleeting concept. The average time for which a share is now held? Some say 22 seconds, some say 11 seconds. Less than a minute in any case, because of high-frequency automated trading. And the speed of trading? It takes a human eye at least 100 milliseconds to blink, but it takes less than a tenth of that time for a trade to travel between Chicago and New York (Lewis 2014, pp. 9ff.). Sticking to the romance that the shareholder is a nice old bloke who founded the company just drives short-termism: in an attempt to keep him in socks by keeping the share price high, companies neglect wider issues of governance and accountability by ignoring other company stakeholders. This mythology has fuelled the exponential rise of boardroom pay, and an overly narrow measurement of corporate performance. But, a bit like Santa Claus, the threat of The Shareholder is still used to make everyone behave.

Seventh, 98 per cent of companies in the UK use a limited liability business model. The dominance of this model is extremely risky. In a global economy, the resilience of the system will always depend on diversity, so no one single model should prevail. This particular model institutionalizes moral hazard, and plays into an increasingly irresponsible shareholder culture, because there is no downside for them. Shareholding executives can afford to take huge risks because they have no liability for debts, and stand only to lose the value of their shareholding. More encouragement in law and public policy of alternative models for enterprise would introduce healthy 'competition' between business models. And more employee ownership and mutualization would spread risk, as well as creating a wider range of businesses with different risk profiles and models of success.

These core assumptions undeniably worked well in capitalism's infancy. But things have moved on, and they are now well past their sell-by date, and are becoming toxic to the system as a whole. The big seven are competition, the invisible hand, the assumption of utility, the assumption that market pricing is just, the assumption of agency theory, the assumption of the supremacy of the shareholder, and the assumption of the primacy of the limited liability model. In each case, these assumptions have become flawed. From a Christian point of view, these flaws are not just operational errors, but grave injustices.

First, humans are made in the image of God, and are given stewardship over creation for the good of the whole of creation. Economics, or 'the running of the household', is therefore seen by Christians as a sacred trust, not a dismal science. While, on the face of it, competition appears an optimal strategy because it aims to improve outcomes over time, the costs of it are too great. Squandering information by hoarding it is wasteful, and reduces the possibility of enhanced outcomes. While game-playing might enable the exercise of God-given intelligence, making it the default approach to economic life privileges ego over outcome, to the dis-benefit of creation as a whole. A bias towards the male of the species is also unacceptable to most people, Christian or not. What would a regulatory and business context based on 'cooperate where you can: compete where you must' look like?

Second, the invisible hand looks Christian, in that it borrows from the idea of divine providence. And while many Christians still believe in some sort of benign fate, the gift of free will carries with it the responsibility of its exercise. This argues against a laissez-faire attitude, particularly one which has been shown to advantage the rich and powerful at the expense of the poor and vulnerable, and of the planet's resources more generally. How could the poor's full participation in the marketplace be accelerated and the rich's tempered to restore justice?

Third, 'utility' encourages an impoverished interpretation of the nature and destiny of humankind. Our Trinitarian God has created us out of and into relationship. A short-term transactional and competitive frame makes us adversaries not brothers and sisters. God has also designed us richly and not as automata, and the complexity of our decision-making is still only partially understood. That we have a capacity and calling to be selfless is a cornerstone of Christian belief, so the selfishness of Economic Man is a travesty. What would a corporate strategy genuinely based on maximizing human flourishing mean for the culture and results of organizations?

Fourth, market pricing. Again, laissez-faire is actually a vote for the powerful, because their wealth allows them to dominate the market, which adapts itself to meet their needs. Allowing pricing to be manipulated by the powerful pollutes the entire marketplace by crowding out other important signals. And Christians as stewards cannot ignore the issue of actual costs, just pricing and externalities. This assumption is perhaps the trickiest to unpick, because history suggests that nation states distort prices as badly as do unfettered markets. But transparency and disclosure about costs, margins and impacts – even in the subsidiaries of subsidiaries – would allow consumers to make better choices about which products and services to buy. Why can't corporates publish breakdowns of their costs, margins and impacts more transparently?

Fifth, agency theory, which would appear justified because of original sin. Christ's sacrifice paid this debt, and there is no room for such a stunted reading of human nature in Christian theology. God gave us the ultimate freedom, and it does violence to the very essence of the Christian story to assume the recalcitrance of human beings. Of course we incline to sin, but structuring it in just encourages it, creating a race to the bottom that is fundamentally dehumanizing. How might a glass half-full approach, coupled with visibility, encourage better behaviour?

Sixth, the narrow view that the shareholder's rights trump all others is an affront to the notion of stewardship. It trivializes the human endeavour bound up in an organization, and encourages an arms-length approach to responsibility. The only Christian way to view the aim of an organization is to look at its contribution to human and planetary flourishing. The culture of greed inculcated by the twin evils of agency theory and shareholder value is deeply sinful. Why are we hanging on to this model, and what would need to happen for it to be dismissed as a flat-earth philosophy?

Seventh, limited liability, as a model, structures moral hazard into the system and schools executives in irresponsibility. A Christian reading of the situation argues in favour of a more democratic approach to ownership; one that recognizes more fully the contribution and role of employees, who are made in the image of God, and are exercising their God-given talents in the workplace. Given that the results of shared ownership speak for themselves, what is really stopping more companies from migrating to this model?

These themes, of human nature, freedom, responsibility, and the protection of the vulnerable, point towards an economy that needs to be more careful about people. The test of its health is the health of every single relationship, customer, supplier, employer, employee, neighbour, environment. And because capitalism is what is called a complex adaptive system, it is fragile and responsive. This makes it readily susceptible to nudges, particularly those by the consumers that provide the demand messages within it. The fact that the system is just a massive complex of relationships and transactions is a huge opportunity for Christians. Christians are estimated to control $10 trillion around the world. At least 6 per cent of the world's investment capital is reckoned to be in the hands of religious bodies. In England, the Church Commissioners alone have an asset portfolio of £7.9 billion, while collectively Anglican PCCs are estimated to spend over £800 million a year. And there are a lot of us. Over 1 million people go to a Church of England church, and 1 in 4 primary schools are run by the Church of England, teaching 1 million children each year. There are still 26 Bishops in the House of Lords, and 20,000 Church of England clergy active in their local communities. This represents a lot of muscle that should be mobilized in shops and online; in policy and in education; in businesses, and in the investment community.

Before we return to a discussion on why and how Christians might act as the salt and light within this system in order to redeem it, we should look in more detail at the essence of consumerism.

Consumerism

If capitalism is the context, consumerism is its daily routine. But how did this term emerge? Kenneth Himes usefully tracks its etymology, and the evolution from a parlance of 'customer' to 'consumer'. As the word derives from the Latin, meaning 'to devour, waste, exhaust', its traditional meaning was wholly negative. Indeed it was used to describe tuberculosis, with the heroines of *La Boheme* and *La Traviata* both famously dying of consumption. But in the eighteenth century the word started to be used by political economists without this negative cast, most famously by Adam Smith in his 1776 classic *Wealth of Nations*. In this usage, a *consumer* was distinguished from a *producer*, and *consumption* became the counterpart to *production*. Later, the word became commonly accepted as a replacement for *customer* as the buyer or purchaser of goods (Himes 2007, pp. 132ff.). Many have seen this move away from a language of customer – with its connotations of relationship – towards a language of consumer as epitomizing the increasingly selfish and destructive nature of modern capitalism.

In 1999, Naomi Klein's *No Logo* hit the bestseller list, summing up for a generation their unease about corporate manipulation of consumers. Subtitled *Taking Aim at the Brand Bullies*, Klein documents the invasion of global brand advertising into every corner of our lives (No Space), the effect this has had on our agency and wellbeing (No Choice), and its impact on the labour market (No Jobs). She concludes with 'No Logo', a call to arms that has been taken up by waves of global anti-capitalist protesters ever since. Her thesis has only intensified with time. Throughout the noughties our unfettered consumer desire was both fuelled and stoked by the ubiquitous availability of credit, until it became apparent that this credit was unsecured, and in 2008 the system famously crashed. We are still climbing out of that particular hole, and what has most materially added to the problem that *No Logo* so pertinently identified is the surge in social media and digital marketing in the years since. The techniques behind this will be discussed later on, but the phenomenon is such that we are now overwhelmed with messaging. As Martin Hilbert's work has shown, in 2011 we took in five times as much information every day as we did in 1986 – the equivalent of 175 newspapers per person per day (Hilbert 2012). And much of this information is either direct advertising or indirect data about what our chosen peer groups and role models are currently consuming. This is already leading to disastrous mental health in teens, who are subjected to relentless daily comparison through social media sites on their smartphones.

It is hard to be objective about consumerism when in the West it is the very air we breathe. So I was particularly lucky to be taken out of this context by a trip to Beijing in 2007. I was escorting a group of MBA students there for a study tour, during which they offered consultancy to some local businesses. My group's client was one of China's top three children's apparel manufacturers, which also retails through stores, catalogues and online. What was fascinating to us was that there was no age differentiation in their range (apart from babywear), and there was little gender distinction. Used to the consumer West, with its aggressive segmentation and relentless pink versus blue, we felt obliged to recommend that they adopt a more differentiated approach. Further, their advertising struck us as intriguing. In their photoshoot, they only used as models classically blond and blue-eyed Western children. While their market was entirely Chinese, they said that aspirational parents wanted their children to look like Western children, hence the campaign. There was also no channel strategy, and their brand strategy was generally to license retro popular culture brands from the West once their value there had declined.

This snapshot was a great way to throw our consumer society into sharp relief as we touched down at Heathrow Airport a few days later. HSBC has a monopoly on the hoardings as you disembark. While HSBC is a bank, one would be hard-pressed to divine this from the walls, which rather deliberately look like an advert for the UN, to signal responsible global citizenship as a key brand message. Then as you enter the arrivals hall the other adverts start, and are continued through every inch of your journey back into London – tube adverts, taxi adverts, bus adverts, train adverts, and even adverts on bicycles; roadside billboards, in-vehicle TV screens, adverts on your smartphone, more adverts on the backs of your tickets and receipts, logos projected into the sky, and adverts painted on roofs. And everyone you meet is a walking advert for their chosen brands – bedecked with logos on clothing and accessories and on what they carry and use. And all with one common aim: to persuade you to buy things, by showing you what kind of life you could have if you did.

A rather intriguing angle on the matter comes from The Skinners' Company, which is one of the Great Twelve livery companies of London, incorporated by Royal Charter in 1327. It was their Beadle who explained to me the complexities of sumptuary law. Have you ever wondered how Cinderella got into that ball without an invitation? Because she obeyed the dress code, courtesy of her Fairy Godmother. Dress codes, or sumptuary laws, have ancient roots. In Rome, only the Emperor or the senators were permitted to wear purple, because the dye used to create Tyrian purple was so highly prized. Similarly, in China, only the Emperor could wear yellow. Elizabeth I was keen on sumptuary law, and her laws were very specific. For example, as at 15 June 1574, fur could only be worn by those worth over 300 marks a year, and even then they could only wear pine-marten, grey civet or lamb-skin. If you wanted to upgrade to grey furs, you had to be earning over £100 a year, or be the son of a knight. Then there was a progressive hierarchy – with fines payable for faking it – through leopard (ambassadors and knights) and lynx (dukes, marquises, earls, viscounts and barons) to sable (the Royal Family).

Whether by diktat or volition, humans have been using appearance and accessories to signal status for as long as folk-lore and archaeology can tell; neither are we alone as a species in so doing. The reason terms like 'alpha male' and 'pecking order' have entered the lexicon is because of how we have observed other species doing status. Darwin's blue-footed booby birds were born like that, plumage, size and colour all being part of nature's design, but aspirational bearded vultures use make-up, rubbing themselves in soil to make them look as reddish-brown as the older and more socially dominant birds. Some animals use objects as status symbols, too. The male gentoo penguin presents his loved one with a carefully chosen perfect pebble for their nest, and the bower bird decorates his nest with brightly coloured objects like shells and treasure to show his superiority as a potential mate. High-status black kites use white plastic to line their nests, and researchers found that when white plastic is placed in lower-status kite nests, they immediately remove it in panic about the insubordination it represents (see Sergio *et al.* 2011).

And at least since Catullus first lied about having Bythinian litter bearers, humans have always tried to keep up with the Joneses. It is such a British trope that the BBC made a famously long-running sitcom about it, *Keeping Up Appearances*. So when in 1899 Thorstein Veblen coined the phrase 'conspicuous consumption', he was labelling a very well-known phenomenon, not discovering anything new. Admittedly, affluence facilitates it, but the phenomenon itself is as old as the hills. Its psychology will be examined in more detail in the next section, together with an insight into the theology of desire.

Meanwhile, the effect of consumerism is to future-proof capitalism. It is the logic that keeps the system in play, by generating on-going demand which ever needs fresh supply. While there are organizations who have invested in supplying this demand, there will be an incentive for them to do everything possible to further this interdependence. And because humans are social animals, there is no realistic prospect of this logic ever breaking down. Even in less affluent societies, we see its emerging power. The grey market globally for hand-me-downs and fakes still privileges the trophies of the developed world, because global communications has now established global demand for elite brands. Dystopian literature paints a picture of what the world might be like without the current privileges many people enjoy; but still in these futures people find ways to use consumption to signal status, even if the resources they have to do so are somewhat different. So is it realistic to fight against this entrenched reality of societal life?

Now that we have examined the relationship between capitalism and consumerism, it is time to look at those theological and secular accounts that attempt to explain their dynamics, and that offer an answer to this vital question.

6

What does God Think About It?

Theological Commentary

Consumerism is not news to theologians (see Himes 2007). While few have engaged with it in a sustained and detailed way, many have muttered darkly about it as being the devil spawn of capitalism, which introduces a permanent cancer into the gene pool. Thus many commentators and preachers have just assumed that God would not approve (see for example many of those writing within the Radical Orthodoxy tradition). Their general argument tends to be that the Powers are taking advantage of our sinful natures to enslave us, and we will never be free while we remain in thrall to them. To remain pure we must opt out, or seek to transcend these dark forces. Nevertheless there are persistent strands in the literature that attend to the reality that consumerism comes freighted with religion and is not independent of it. Indeed, their correspondence is both the problem and the solution. As William Cavanaugh argues, 'Consumerism is an important subject for theology because it is a spiritual disposition, a way of looking at the world around us that is deeply formative' (Cavanaugh 2008, p. 35) Vincent Miller agrees: 'Consumer culture poses a particularly vexing problem for Christianity because the shape and texture of the desires that it cultivates are profoundly similar to Christian forms of desire' (Miller 2005, p. 107). As these kinds of treatments offer more therapeutic and engaging remedies than the austerity of seclusion, these will be the focus of the discussion that follows.

One of the seminal thinkers on consumerism is Colin Campbell from the University of York. In his 1987 book *The Romantic*

Ethic and the Spirit of Modern Consumerism he draws out the
three essential components of consumerism, being insatiability,
novelty and subjectivity. The first two interact with each other
to drive consumerism, because nothing is new for long, and
obtaining something merely triggers longing for the next new
thing, ad infinitum. The component of subjectivity is linked to
day-dreaming and our personal aspirations in life. Yes, influenced by peer groups, advertising and fashion, but also person-
alized as an individual volition to consume (Campbell 2005,
pp. 36–43, 85f.). But what really makes consumerism different
from mere hedonistic pleasure-seeking is its insatiability. This
infinity of longing is what reveals consumerism as a proto-
spirituality, because by definition it can never be satisfied. As
Marx famously remarked, consumer goods are fetish objects: their
value transcends their material utility. They are the means, not the
end. Their desirability is a function of their capacity to mediate
value (McGrath 2014, p. 5 n.17). This means that, contrary to
the popular view, consumerism is not about material goods at all.
The material cannot satisfy an existential longing, but pretends to,
by promising satisfaction. This is what generates the restlessness
that characterizes modern capitalism, and acts as a ratchet on it,
generating unending demand that requires to be supplied.

As the Newfoundland academic Sean McGrath notes:

> The key to the endlessness of consumer desire is the absolute
> futurity of its object: the consumer always projects the desired
> into the future, for only thus is it safe from the disappoint-
> ment of reality. It matters little if the object or the experience
> is genuinely new or not; all that matters is that the imagina-
> tion of the consumer renders it so. The consumer imagines the
> desired to be something new, something not yet enjoyed. And
> the genius of consumerism is that no amount of real-world dis-
> appointment can divest the consumer of his or her dream, for
> what is sought is not the thing but the way of being which
> the thing makes possible, i.e., an imagined experience, not an
> actual object. Consumer disappointment – more essential to
> keeping the economy moving than consumer enjoyment – is the

consumer's inevitable discovery that what he or she imagined as a fresh avenue to self-fulfillment was not in fact significantly different from previous acquisitions and conquests and does not deliver the desired transformation of the self. But far from quenching the fire of consumer desire, the disappointment only fans the flames. A rationalization for the disappointment lies ready-to-hand: the fault lies in the thing that proves inadequate to the desire, not in the desire itself. Consumerism lives out of the 'not yet', and insofar as its goal is the possible rather than the actual, it can pursue it infinitely. (McGrath 2014, p. 18)

Commenting on Campbell, McGrath notices behind his three essential features an inversion of the classic virtues of faith, hope and love. Faith leads to personal spirituality, by teaching us that we can all individually have a relationship with God and are individually special to him. Hope delays gratification, by teaching us that fulfilment lies ever in the future. Love fuels our drive to be accepted and acceptable, fed in the marketplace by lifestyle advertising. This erodes communitarianism, de-prioritizes resolution, and persuades us that our desires are essentially altruistic, thereby creating the perfect conditions for consumerism: 'Christian spirituality, inverted and in disavowal of its origins, produces the perfect capitalist machine, a system of infinite demand' (p. 22). In the absence of any belief in God, 'subjectivity finds only bottomless emptiness in itself, a need that nothing can fill, and so is driven to endlessly reproduce itself by, at all costs, keeping desire alive, even when the object desired is proven time and again to be a deception, a lie, yet another piece of consumer junk' (p. 16).

Rowan Williams echoes this analysis when he talks about this restless search for completion through 'things'. He challenges this impoverished mentality as one which, in Christian terms, totally underestimates the nature of grace. Grace does not simply gratify and will overflow any neat hole that we expect it to fill. The feeding of the 5,000 is a good illustration of this: the five loaves and the two fish feed the multitude, yet the scraps left over still fill 12 baskets. Williams argues that it is childish to imagine that we are on the verge of completion, and that the latest gadget, accessory or experience will make us – finally – happy. Consumerism plays into a narrative that imagines we just have a few neat gaps left that the market will fill for us, at a price. For Williams, growing up requires us to stop desiring the end of desire, and to come to terms with the incurable character of our desire. Nothing on earth should satisfy us. We are designed to be restless until we find our rest in God, so we should embrace this yearning in our character. Instead of trying to put an end to it, we should instead long only for 'a steady and endless enlarging of the heart' through God's overflowing grace, and through others who might offer us unexpected transformation and growth. It is in desiring grace that we are most likely to find peace, so he would agree with Gregory of Nyssa, who says in his *Life of Moses* that never to reach satiety of desire is truly to see God (Williams 2000b, p. 153; Williams 2002, p. 243). As William Schweiker puts it, 'the love of God can limit the desire for acquisition precisely because what is desired exceeds objectification' (Schweiker 2004, p. 269).

Richard Harries would introduce the seventeenth-century theologian Thomas Traherne into the argument at this point, to reinforce the point about the right ordering of desire. He turns to Traherne to examine whether desire might actually be the proper starting point for Christians. Traherne argues that, because God is so prone to give, 'it is of the nobility of man's soul that he is insatiable . . . the noble inclination whereby man thirsteth after riches and dominion, is his highest virtue, when rightly guided' (Harries 1992, p. 79).

Other theologians have developed this essential theme of desire and restlessness, captured by William Cavanaugh in this passage:

> Consumers are characterized by a constant dissatisfaction with material goods. This dissatisfaction is what produces the restless pursuit of satisfaction in the form of something new. Consumerism is not so much about having more as it is about having something else; that's why it is not simply *buying* but *shopping* that is at the heart of consumerism. Buying brings a temporary halt to the restlessness that typifies consumerism. This restlessness – the moving on to shopping for something else, no matter what one has just purchased – sets the spiritual tone for consumerism (Cavanaugh 2008, p. 35).

And Charles Mathewes is particularly concerned about where this warping of desire might end, in thrall to Mammon. He argues that we use consumerism to avoid life rather than to inhabit it:

> This is finally idolatrous, for it reveals both that our attachment to certain goods in the world is always threatening to become a worshipful attachment, and that behind this counterfeit worship lies an even deeper idolatry, the commitment to the mastery of the world by the self, the desire to make the self its own god – or rather, to have no other gods before the self. (Mathewes 2012, p. 14)

The theologian who has best captured the nub of the problem, though, is Peter Sedgwick. His vital contribution to the debate is to explain that consumerism is essentially a search for self-identity (Sedgwick 1999, pp. 95f.). He traces its roots to a Christian ethic of pleasure derived from Arminianism and the Cambridge Platonists, and tracks its evolution from Sentimentalism through Romanticism to the present day. In doing so, he identifies its central paradox: 'the irony is that this search for identity destroys itself, for the infinity of desire cannot be satisfied' (p. 133, see also pp. 83ff., 86–8). If the final triumph of consumerism is that it has become the ultimate search for self-identity, it also renders it morally empty. Removing desire from its theological context and replacing it with a secular narrative of consumerism makes even social action more about self-interest than about altruism. Consumerism as a selfish search for identity quickly becomes vocational, and its very limitlessness has become dangerous not only for our collective mental health but for the health of the planet as a whole. Sedgwick would agree that consumerism has been allowed to become a 'competing desire' in opposition to Christianity, but not very consciously so, nor irreparably.

But why is desire part of our design as God's people? An answer to this question is located in the theodicy of John Hick (Hick 1985). His articulation of life as the 'vale of soul-making' evocatively explains the theological predicament. In the act of creation, God necessarily alienated us from his presence. He spun us out

86

so that we might genuinely be other. But this 'epistemic distance', designed to protect our free will, makes us yearn to come home, and be reunited with our creator. This longing was most succinctly put at the very start of the *Confessions* of St Augustine of Hippo: 'Thou hast made us for thyself, O Lord, and our heart is restless until it finds its rest in thee.' This is the impetus behind the traditions of theosis or deification in the spirituality of many of the world's religions, which try to chart a specific course back to God. But for those of us not at liberty to retreat to a monastery, can we satisfy our desires here on earth, or must we patiently await death? Into the vacuum strides consumerism, with the promise that its brands can indeed help us achieve final happiness this side of Eden. But we know – from a rehearsal of both the psychology and the physiology of consumption – that we can never be satisfied with 'things', because they far too quickly become un-novel through familiarity and copying, and therefore redundant.

Thus the core vulnerability that consumerism finds easy to exploit is human anxiety. Many have written about the seeming rise in anxiety in the modern world. While we cannot know for sure whether we are indeed more anxious these days, we certainly have myriad ways both to identify anxiety and to measure it, as well as to spread global alarm about it (e.g. James 2007 and 2008). Tim Jackson has written about anxiety in the context of consumerism, and notes the role religion has traditionally played in addressing human anxiety. Drawing on the work of Peter Berger, he describes Berger's concept of the 'sacred canopy', or the explanatory narrative that religions provide to help humans make sense both of their lives and of their concerns about living. Religion does so by providing cognitive, emotional and moral meaning, and the many empirical studies that suggest a link between religion and wellbeing would suggest that it does so rather well (Spencer *et al.* 2016). In societies that are secularizing, where religion ceases to fulfil this function, consumerism can seemingly provide an alternative. But consumerism is flawed as an explanatory narrative because it has no telos. It has no eschatology, because to do so would cap spending at some point in the future, undermining the economic cycle and growth (Jackson 2013, pp. 55ff.).

Secular Commentary

We leave the theologians, noticing that consumerism is a response to what appears to be a spiritual yearning, but a response that operates under the false promise that it can satisfy this need, and one that in fact seems to undermine human happiness. Alongside these theological accounts lie the (ostensibly) secular ones. I consider these methodologically in parallel because of what they might add to the theological account, on the Rabbi Jonathan Sacks view that if you believe in divine revelation, you must be open to the idea that God might reveal himself through other people's truths too.

From the theological account, we have already identified desire as pivotal, but if we step into the stream of capitalism as it currently is, the banks on either side can be seen as a call and response between supply and demand. The insatiable desiring of consumers identified by the theologians has been met in late-stage capitalism by an increasingly sophisticated consumer brand response. Because novelty and satisfaction are incompatible and infinite, consumerism bakes in a ratchet that guarantees long-term revenue streams, which are likely to increase exponentially over time, given the logic and therefore relative scarcity of both novelty and satisfaction. To properly understand this phenomenon, therefore, we must examine both desire and branding.

Desire

It was René Girard who in 1961 introduced the theory of 'mimetic desire' to explain human behaviour. He argued that we learn by copying not just the behaviour of those that surround us, but also their desires. In his thinking, this inevitably creates tension and violence, which is of course self-evident to anyone who has had twins or looked after toddlers, who always want what the other has, and will fight them for it. In an empiricist age, scientists would like Girard to have collected more data on this front; but there is ample data to be found post hoc in the vast consumer machine that now runs on this logic. And do you recall the Dr Seuss story about the Sneetches? There are Star-Belly Sneetches and Plain-Belly Sneetches. One day, an entrepreneur comes to town with a machine. The plain-bellies give him cash, and he puts a star on their bellies. Then he charges the outraged star-bellies to have their stars removed; then the newly starred to have theirs removed, then the original stars to be replaced, and so forth and so on, until he leaves them in disarray, a very rich man.

Advertisers, having started off simply presenting pictures of the product they wanted you to buy, have migrated towards a highly successful strategy that involves showing you who you could become if you invest in their product, first by the use of aspirational models, and latterly through celebrity endorsement. The effect of both of these manoeuvres, and the ubiquity of advertising, has been an increase in eating disorders and cosmetic surgery, and a new market in male cosmetics. The rise in the use of celebrity endorsement has also delivered a brand bonanza, where Waitrose sells out of cranberries if Delia Smith uses them, and the James Bond movies are financed as a deliberate extended advertisement for premium lifestyle accessories. Girard's concern that mimetic desire can morph into the fatal desire to become the other is also the plot-line in films like *The Talented Mr Ripley* and *Single White Female*.

A famous study on vervet monkeys provides a chemical explanation for why this habit may become so ingrained. The experiments (McGuire and Raleigh 1985) found that high-ranking male vervets had nearly twice as much serotonin in their blood as those ranking lower in the social hierarchy. If an alpha male was displaced by a challenger, his serotonin levels would plummet, until he was able to reassert his status in the troop. And this is what happens when someone buys the latest 'thing'. When their social group signals their approval, they get a burst of serotonin, and this becomes addictive because if they don't keep 'on top' they will quite literally feel depressed. And in this selfie-obsessed age, it is a tragic irony that McGuire and Raleigh's research showed the only other way to crash vervet serotonin was to maroon a senior monkey with only a mirror for company.

No wonder social media is having such a deleterious effect on mental health. Facebook is like a vast troop of vervet monkeys, giving you instant and repeated feedback about your status in your social group. This restlessness is now turbo-charged by pings from phones. If you don't get affirmation, you suffer the same fate as the monkey with the mirror, and start feeling anxious about your status. With the ubiquity of smartphones and social media, new data has come to light about the effects of this social activity on mental health, particularly for young people (Twenge 2017). Many schools are now banning smartphone use. In France, a total ban on pupils using mobile phones in both primary and secondary schools started in September 2018.

As was earlier noted in the discussion of Martin Hilbert's work on information, while it would be unwise to conflate smartphones with consumerism, they are increasingly the primary source of consumer messaging. Further, they may overstimulate desire because of the effect the technology has on dopamine. What the 'liking' technology achieves is an escalation in the volume of 'comparison events' such that we are now more regularly aware of how we compare to others in our self-curated social groups. If we have alerts switched on, every time someone in our social group interacts, we are informed. If something we do attracts positive feedback (views, likes and comments) we feel good and want to repeat the experience to feel good again in the future. It is this positive feedback loop, powered by dopamine, that is so problematic, because while dopamine is implicated in 'liking', its function is to stimulate 'wanting' to motivate us to continue to seek out positive things in the future (Berridge and Robinson 1998). So our natural psychological tendency to seek satisfaction through visible consumption, designed to attract positive social reinforcement, is actually encouraged by our body chemistry. This means that social media is to consumerism what consumerism is to capitalism, and this unholy trinity binds us into a maelstrom of desiring that is tragically destined to fail to satisfy.

And what exactly is it that we desire? Kenneth Himes identifies three categories of consumer desire: desire for material welfare (physical needs for clothing, food, shelter); desire for display (Veblen's conspicuous consumption); and desire for psychic well-being (security, leisure) (Himes 2007, p. 138). This is reminiscent of the famous hierarchy of needs proposed by Abraham Maslow (Maslow 1943), which suggests that there is a progression from the first to the third of these. In his language, once we have met our basic physiological needs, for example for food, we will seek safety (shelter), then social belonging (in-groups), then self-esteem, then finally self-actualization and transcendence (spiritual fulfilment). Early analyses of consumer desires were quite specific, with US consumer fantasies centring on new and better homes, new cars and luxury items like jewellery and designer clothes. John Caughey expanded these desires into seven categories: career success, alternative career success, natural world escape, material wealth, successful violence, sex-romance, and blissful married life (Beaudoin 2003, p. 52). But both of these lists reflect earlier stages of consumerism, where advertising in its infancy focused on products and services rather than the person you could become through acquiring them. Nowadays, as we will see below, marketers know that the logic of Maslow suggests an approach that is as aspirational as possible, and goes beyond even the in-group and esteem stages towards self-actualization, in line with Peter Sedgwick's observation about self-identity.

And it is in noticing this progression, and marrying the insights of theology and psychology, that we begin to see the potential for the redemption of consumerism. But first, how has the market attempted to address consumer desire?

Branding

Busy worrying about our immortal souls, perhaps we have not noticed the spiritual journey that the corporations we love to hate have been embarked upon all along. When the Industrial Revolution started, there grew up an organizational support system to package, distribute and sell the products made. Over time, and with increasing sophistication, sales and marketing developed into a discipline that was less about trying very hard to sell products already made, and more about creating goods and services that consumers actually wanted, adopting a market-based pricing strategy that chimed in with this market-led strategy. The discipline of listening to customers and responding to them evolved into a strategy that focused increasingly on brands, and far less on the products and services that carried their insignia. A good example of this progression is Nike. Originally called Blue Ribbon Sports, it began with the founders selling Japanese sports shoes out of the back of their cars at sports games. They moved on to manufacturing their own, with the help of a waffle iron, and were early adopters of advertising that was less about the shoes and more about what they enabled you to do. The famous Nike swoosh logo was established, and celebrity endorsement from the likes of Michael Jordan and Tiger Woods meant that their logo was in demand as a status symbol, facilitating an expansion into sports apparel and leisurewear. Now their vast flagship Niketown stores invite you to customize your own clothes and shoes, which you can also do globally online. Nike is now the world's largest supplier of athletic shoes and apparel, and the world's most valuable sports brand.

As Naomi Klein famously identified in *No Logo*, companies increasingly see themselves as 'meaning brokers' not as mere product or service producers. She notes that the big brands have sloughed off their physical bodies, and emerged in a more spiritual realm, because anyone can manufacture a product, leaving the Head Office increasingly free 'to focus on the real business at hand – creating a corporate mythology powerful enough to infuse meaning into these raw objects just by signing its name' (Klein 2001, p. 22). Cynically, of course, this is also used to create legal distance between the brand and its supply chain, particularly where this has become morally problematic.

Either way, this distillation of the relationship permits 'brand stretching' so that the logo can reasonably be applied to any product or service that could also deliver on the brand promise.

We see this simplistically in supermarkets, with shelves full of own-branded goods, but we also see these supermarkets branching out into other businesses, like banking, because they can argue for consistency of promise. The most famous example of brand stretching is Richard Branson's Virgin brand. It started as Virgin Records in 1970, Branson initially selling records by post before opening a store on Oxford Street in London. Next, he set up Virgin Atlantic, an airline competing with BA on transatlantic flights. Mates condoms, Virgin Radio, Virgin Brides, Virgin Cosmetics and Virgin Cola followed. Later, Virgin Trains, Virgin Mobile, Virgin Active, Virgin Galactic and Virgin Bank. Currently, the Virgin logo adorns planes, trains, spaceships, cruise ships, hotels, health clubs, money, media, radio, music and sports festivals across the world. The old logic was that you expanded into those other markets where either you could achieve scale or leverage know-how: but Virgin is just one example of a global brand that could feasibly be attached to just about anything. The brand promise is about being less stuffy than the competition, so any industry with tired players is fair game. And this extraordinary ability to badge wildly different goods or services shows that branding is nothing to do with those goods and services, and everything to do with the customer relationship. Being a Mac person rather than a PC person has more to do with the Apple brand and consumer loyalty to its values than it has to do with commercial decisions about functionality or price.

What Nike, Apple and other mega brands do well is to realize that brand is about relationship, so it is about emotion. Lesser brands like Tesco tend to average back to being commodity brands, because they fail to understand this vital point. Motivational slogans like *Just Do It*, and social campaigning by brands, inspire both affiliation and loyalty way beyond anything that could be generated simply through value-for-money transactions. And for businesses this reduces the cost of sales, it increases wallet-share, and generates sticky customers who will generate annuity returns for years to come. While traditional product marketing is about differentiating your products from other products, brand marketing is about differentiating your customers from other customers. Providing a story and an identity creates a tribe, and an in-group who will increasingly have a stake in your success, because it now connotes their success too. As Beaudoin puts it, branding is about offering membership of a community. 'Branding also offers a consistent, coherent identity, in which you are told about your true self . . . there is a way of life, an identity, that can be had by participating in the logo-centric economy' (Beaudoin 2003, p. 44). A colleague of mine once bumped into another colleague in Tesco. Horrified, her colleague blurted out, 'I normally shop at Waitrose!' which beautifully illustrates this point.

Branding is fascinating to a theologian, because it borrows heavily from the language of trust, belief and covenant. At the heart of every brand is the famous brand promise, that if you buy our goods and services you will receive a consistent customer experience, like Disney = fun, Volvo = safe, and IKEA = affordable. And rather than railing against this, perhaps religious communities need to recognize that this is what religions have always done, too. In fact, they invented it. The wisdom traditions have always used stories, tools and rituals to draw people into community, to create structures of meaning and purpose, as well as to worship the divine. While the anti-capitalist commentators are right that consumerism is a travesty of true religion, it is the religious communities who have let this happen, by failing to provide a stronger competing narrative.

Theology of Consumerism

From this discussion, it is possible to draw out an emerging theology about consumerism. To work, consumerism requires desire. So does faith. Both programmes use the same operating system. Consumerism promises fulfilment, but leads to disappointment. Faith does not promise completion in this life, so does not build in or require perennial disappointment to drive it in the same way.

Consumerism can have positive effects, but by design leads to the over-consumption of scarce resources and to mental distress. In contrast, faith offers a journey back to God, so can be the only true fulfilment for humankind. Moreover, faith offers a wholesome alternative that is more other-directed and community-spirited, so proves therapeutic both for the individual and society.

The ancient faith traditions have stood the test of time. Our ancestors handed them down to us because they were found to be of value. And Christianity in particular is well placed to lead the response to consumerism, because the centrality of Christ's death and resurrection offers consolation to a creation transfixed by death. Protestant Christianity's emphasis on *sola fides* restores virtue to the heart of human morality, because it prioritizes being over doing – albeit in the hope that the former drives excellence in the latter – thereby rescuing humanity from the requirement to display achievement as religious signalling. The rhythms of Christian belief can offer an alternative routine that puts consumerism back into perspective. While the technologies of consumerism are sophisticated, so too are the conventions of religion. Currently the faith communities are not heard as loudly in the marketplace, and do not have the societal footfall of old, so reach is restricting audibility. But that is the only problem. Christianity has the answers, and is already hard at work. The central challenge is to amplify this message so as to proclaim a more visible alternative to consumerism.

7

What Should We do About It?

Self-fulfilling Prophecies?

There is a whiff of fatalism about consumerism, because it is ana-
lysed and described by the social scientists. The economic models
they use assume that outcomes are generally predictable, based
on past performance. But such models should always be treated
with suspicion when they involve humans and not machines.
In economic theory it is the classic confusion between what is
called 'positive' and 'normative' economics. Positive economics is largely descriptive ('eight out of ten cats prefer Whiskas'),
while normative economics is prescriptive (all cats should – or
indeed will – prefer Whiskas). It has become normal to confuse
the two by assuming that what is ought also to be. Many commentators worry that this habit – as well as being mistaken –
leads to moral corrosion, as it tends to round down to the lowest
common denominator. If 'research' shows that most people lie,
does it not follow that it is 'normal' to do so, and therefore no
longer 'wrong'?

This kind of persistently deterministic thinking, particularly in
a group context, naturally becomes suggestive. This is because
it normalizes behaviours to the extent that fresh deliberation is
seemingly no longer required, and 'everyone's doing it' becomes
a universal justification. Apart from the obvious issue of the
future being unknown, the idea that the future – and human
activity within it – can be confidently predicted through the past
is a counsel of despair and denies free will. So I want to start by
the strong assertion that consumerism is susceptible to change,

because humans are, and consumerism is a human phenomenon. Having used Niebuhr's famous Christ and Culture typology as a specimen, it is tempting to deploy it here. But while it can usefully frame an approach to addressing consumerism, it is light on the detail. So instead this section will first identify some actions the Church might want to take, then focus on how you as the reader could take up the gauntlet in your daily life.

Church

First, as we have seen, a desire to consume is entirely normal and is not necessarily theologically problematic. This means that it is unhelpful when religious communities simply tell consumers off, unless they can articulate a better alternative. So theologians and religious leaders need to brush up on their theologies of desire, that they might be better placed to win the argument for God, and to wean consumers off an addiction to that which cannot satisfy. Historical examples of the venerable tradition of 'baptizing' the indigenous are legion, whether it be St Patrick in Ireland, Patristic rebranding of classical philosophy, or liberation theology's appropriation of Marx. Modern theologians have also contributed useful labels to describe this practice. After Alasdair MacIntyre, Malcolm Brown calls for us to 'enlarge the narrative', while Ben Quash introduces the notion of 'redescription' (Brown 2004, pp. 198ff.; Quash 2006). Borrowing from the traditions of theatrical improvisation, Sam Wells would call this 'overaccepting', which is about fitting the smaller story into the larger story about what God is doing with the world (Wells 2004, pp. 131ff.). All of these terms seek to describe the activity captured in this passage in Acts 17.22–25:

> Then Paul stood in front of the Areopagus and said, 'Athenians, I see how extremely religious you are in every way. For as I went through the city and looked carefully at the objects of your worship, I found among them an altar with the

inscription, "To an unknown god." What therefore you worship as unknown, this I proclaim to you. The God who made the world and everything in it, he who is Lord of heaven and earth, does not live in shrines made by human hands, nor is he served by human hands, as though he needed anything, since he himself gives to all mortals life and breath and all things.'

In his elegant discussion of consumerism as a search for self-identity, Peter Sedgwick makes a telling point. Criticizing Veblen, he notes that not all consumption is deliberately conspicuous. One might buy books to study alone, or listen to music privately, still in pursuit of self-identity, but not in public view. And while it is the case that humans are a social species, the extent to which individuals crave external approval differs from personality to personality, with some people being more internally referenced than others. If we are clear that the driver is self-identity and not consumption, which is a mere means to that end, we can address the matter more directly, by emphasizing the claims of religion as helper-in-chief on this very human and perennial predicament. Berger's sacred canopy is about religion as a meaning-making construct, but where the Church does not provide meaning, people will seek meaning elsewhere. Cries for 'relevance' generally meet with exasperation from clergy, but it is not so much about being trendy as it is about covering the ground. Do you preach about this kind of thing or not? Because if you don't, your parishioners are getting it from their smartphones instead.

Modern psychological theories like Maslow's hierarchy of needs provide a secular version of what the wisdom traditions have always known: that we are all on a spiritual journey. Capitalism knows this, too, and modern consumerism is as obsessed with meaning and purpose as we are. And that is why we can redeem consumerism. While the neo-liberal capitalist agenda has prioritized shareholder value, lending a relentlessness to profit-seeking and growth that is parasitic, more enlightened versions of capitalism and its organizations know that this is doomed to fail. There are no customers on a dead planet.

Only those organizations that find a middle way between planet and profit will ultimately survive, and while it is a slow process, the wheel is slowly turning. Different ownership structures, changes in governance and accountability, the sustainability agenda, and growing awareness of externalities and global risk are all playing their part, and consumers are helping to push this wheel by increasingly demanding citizenship from the brands they support.

There is a prevailing instinct within Christianity to try to turn away from desire, to somehow withstand its tractor beam and push it back to its source. This is possibly because the word 'desire' attracts Freudian connotations, but in judo you defeat your opponent by using their own strength against them. So rather than competing head-on, or applying Christian therapies like sticking plaster to repair the wounds of consumerism, it is time to reclaim our basic theology of desire, recently colonized by consumerism but not conquered by it. Like Einstein, we should leap upon its beam and go for a fast ride. Desire is part of the human condition, and our spiritual task is not to resist it, but to curve it away from materialism back towards God. This suggests that churches could do more to attend to the spiritual formation of their parishioners. Many do this well, through house groups, Lent groups, Bible study and retreats. The more ordinary Christians are trained in the spiritual disciplines, the more defences they will have against the wiles of consumerism.

In this context, one rather dark explanation for the important contribution Christianity might make to curbing excessive consumerism concerns death. Ernest Becker won a Pulitzer Prize for his 1973 classic *The Denial of Death*, in which he argued that in order to cope with the horror of our mortality, we develop strategies to escape awareness of our vulnerability. In particular, we indulge in distracting activity to establish 'heroic immortality' through the creation of anything that might last, for example, fame, a family, a business, or a contribution to culture. In developing this theme, Arndt *et al.* argue that another way we deal with our terror about death is to go shopping. They contend that one way humans contain their existential anxiety about mortality is to pursue wealth and the acquisition of culturally desired commodities. In their research, the prospect of death heightened materialism in their test subjects, which explains why President Bush's famous exhortation after September 11 for Americans to go shopping was so pertinent (Arndt *et al.* 2003, pp. 198ff.). Becker concludes that the only thing that helps us cope with our fear of death is some kind of metanarrative that keeps our terror at bay. On this logic, he reckons that Christianity is a particularly salient religion because of the centrality of the death and resurrection of Christ. Because it contextualizes death explicitly, as central to the narrative, it removes any taboo about discussing it, and helps manage our terror about death. All religions cater for meaning-making about death, of course, but in Christianity, Good Friday and Easter are central to doctrine.

Interestingly, Arndt *et al.* also conclude that Christianity is the answer to consumerism, for another particular reason. They conclude their analysis by suggesting that the solution to the tendency to find solace in the material is the promotion of the pursuit of intrinsic values (Arndt *et al.*, 2003, p. 210). This of course is a core competence of religion, and particularly of post-Reformation versions of Christianity with their emphasis on *sola fides*. As was argued in the earlier discussion on capitalism, the primacy of an ethic of utilitarianism flies counter to this, so their analysis provides further support for a rediscovery of character and virtue ethics. Accordingly, character will loom large in the discussion that follows.

A further perspective is offered by paying attention to power. As Girard, Veblen and my parable of the Sneetches would suggest, what is desirable is defined by the haves, not the have-nots. It is those who start off with the most power who dictate the rules of the game thereafter. Whether or not the Church feels powerful in a plural society, in England it has the access, the assets and the demographics that mark it out as a Power, and not one of the dispossessed. So how we role model desire is vital, because what we do has power and can set the tone. It is an opportunity for leadership. Meanwhile, the core message of this section is that Christianity is incredibly well placed to rescue humanity from a negative spiral of consumerism, we just need to get a lot better at saying so, showing the way and being heard.

Character

Some would say that consuming ethically is pointless, in terms of impact; and dangerous, because of moral licensing. Our small efforts are pathetic; and good behaviour in our consumption merely encourages us to regard our moral debt as having been paid, freeing us to behave badly in other avenues of life. We should give to charity instead, and outsource our virtue to them. This is the thrust of the argument in an interesting book called *Doing Good Better* by William Macaskill. In it he argues most persuasively for 'effective altruism', which commends a forensic way to search out impact in order to focus effort and investment (Macaskill 2015, pp. 158ff.). There is much to agree with in his thesis. He notes that our attempts to be green and to buy local or fairtrade do not have as much impact as giving the equivalent amount of money to the right charity, because these benefit from both scale and specialism. And in deploying a strategy of donating to charity, it makes sense to pick a charity that is both efficient and effective, and one that targets a meaningful global problem. This leads him to recommend an altruism strategy called 'earning to give', which takes this argument to its logical conclusion: earning as much as you can will optimize the amount of charitable donation deployable in this altruism strategy. Without wishing to denigrate efficient and generous charitable giving, this theory of change is not mine. Neither is it particularly attractive, theologically speaking.

Of course there is a risk that much of our charitable activity is not as effective as it could be, because we may be supporting enterprises that are local, inefficient and domestic in reach. And perhaps sometimes we create more harm than the good we intend, by helping ineffective charities stumble on rather than letting the market wipe them out in favour of their excellent cousins. The effective altruism argument is that if we want to do good, we should give money to charity, because the best charities are most efficiently placed to make the most of any money we might have to spend on altruism. This is of course entirely true, if we have a view of altruism that it is primarily about effecting good, in or for others, through money. And it is true that our feeble and local efforts of in-kind support or volunteering are dwarfed by the organizational might of the NGOs. Perhaps we should indeed pursue the 'earning to give' strategy. After all, it was John Wesley who said: 'earn all you can, give all you can, save all you can'. But this account of altruism ignores virtue, by outsourcing our morality to others. It ignores the role of the benefactor as anything more than a source of funding, and it ignores the important idea of solidarity. This kind of altruism could never truly be called social liturgy. And because the most precious gift we have to give is ourselves, our person should not be neglected in this way. In the context of consumption, giving of our time and talents – as well as any possessions we might accrue – is pivotal to any ethical discussion about it.

This brings us to the important matter of character and its formation. One person who has written extensively about virtue and character in the modern period is Alasdair MacIntyre. In his 1981 book *After Virtue*, he explains behaving virtuously as the difference between doing something for the extrinsic or instrumental rewards it could give you, or doing it just because it is a good thing to do in and of itself. Art for the sake of art. To illustrate this, he uses an analogy of painting. Painting a portrait gives the artist an external reward (payment or fame), but in paying deep attention to its quality and excellence beyond that which might be required to generate this external reward, the artist also contributes to the general professional practice of portrait painting, an internal reward or good-in-itself. And character is the result of virtuous practices, repeated over time.

MacIntyre would describe an act of altruism like giving to charity as 'contingent': you do it because of what you might get back. The charity delivers good outcomes for you, and you feel good about yourself. But MacIntyre would argue that contingency introduces both a level of conditionality and a level of selfishness into your practice. When we meet virtuous people, people of 'good character', there is something durable and reliable about them. Their values are the core of their being. They cannot avoid being virtuous, it is somehow in their DNA. Character has become no longer about doing but about being. It is now not an activity, but an intrinsic property. That is why, when a kind person is catty, we say 'that was out of character'.

We know the power of developing character through practices because we have preserved it in our mythology. All wisdom traditions have tales of trials, where a hero has to be tested and found true. The labours of Hercules, princes slaying dragons, hobbits ring-bearing – each trial represents what Sir Edmund Hillary described when he said: 'it is not the mountain we conquer, but ourselves'. They are what the character expert David Brooks would call those 'crucible moments' when we need to be tried in the fire in order to achieve purity (Brooks 2015, p. 13). And character matters more than ever. This is because we are wholly overwhelmed with information, which forces us to be selective. This means we have to be good at choosing. We need to be grounded in a deep sense of values and purpose so that we do not lose our bearings. We need to make wise choices.

In the literature, character usually shows up as an enthusiastic rediscovery of the Aristotelian idea of virtue ethics. Virtue ethics contrasts with systems of morality based on rules or consequences, on the basis that it is less about obeying laws or playing the odds, and more about durable habits and character traits. It is about virtue for virtue's sake: virtue as its own reward. And virtue ethics is hugely sophisticated, seen retrospectively through the eyes of modern neurobiology. As Aristotle himself puts it in Book Two of his *Nicomachean Ethics*: 'we become just by doing just acts, temperate by doing temperate acts, brave by doing brave acts'. And we now know that this is neurobiologically true: if you change your behaviour, you will rewire your brain.

A man lies injured in the road. A passer-by who has a rule-based morality will help because they believe in a maxim such as 'do as you will be done by', and they would hope to be rescued in a similar plight. A person who lives by an ethic of optimizing outcomes will help, because doing so will improve the lot of the victim, and possibly their own by showing their altruism. Aristotle would help, because to do so would be virtuous, and it would allow him to exercise the moral practice of benevolence or mercy.

Of course, character is built up over time as the cumulative effect of a series of decisions and behaviours, so it could in theory be informed by either a rule- or consequence-based ethic. But the emphasis in virtue ethics is not about the reactive optimizing of individual decision-making, it is about the deliberate and proactive development of moral character. So in fact the deliberate or accidental accumulation of experiences and behavioural templating is actually what we mean when we say 'character'. Like pearls, our lustre, and the beauty of our nature, comes from this defensive softening of irritants through layers of response over time.

This is hard work, but less risky than the alternatives. A person who subscribes to a rule-based morality would improve themselves by getting ever better at learning and interpreting rules. This breeds a degree of legalistic sophistication, but does not help to notice when rules should be revised, renegotiated or virtuously disobeyed. The diligent consequentialist would hone their morality by getting ever better at reading the future to improve their ability to calculate outcomes. This future-scanning is useful, but it extrapolates from the past so can be blind-sided by novelty. It also provides no nourishment when good decisions turn bad. There is some nobility – if also naivety – in obeying a rule even if it leads to failure. But a bad call makes a person look foolish or weak, even if the decision made looked robust at the time.

Working on your character is about proactivity. The virtuous person is not blind to rules or consequences, but does not restrict or confine ethics to them. They do not wait for an ethical dilemma to present itself for resolution, they bake in daily ethical practice so that such events become humdrum and reflexive. David Brooks calls this the pursuit of 'eulogy virtues'. In his book *The Road to Character*, he argues that we have been duped into pursuing 'resumé virtues' instead, but that these are empty if they are not supported by the depth of a good character (2015, p. ix). This may be why it is now fashionable to start MBA programmes by asking participants to write their own eulogy, because inevitably in the final analysis we yearn for plaudits to do with generosity or kindness or love, not just of career success and material wealth.

My Ashridge colleague Chris Nichols uses a metaphor in strategy about whether you are sailing to France or discovering the North-West Passage. In the case of the former, it is on the map; it is a common journey; tides and hazards are largely known. You chart a course and you sail there. Yes, there may be squalls or pirates, but these you can plan for. And that magic line on your map shows you at any time how far off course you have gone and how to correct for your destination. Morality can be similar. Laws and rules of thumb have been developed down the centuries and internationally across the wisdom and legal traditions to give you the best possible framework for known dilemmas and quandaries. The utilitarian tradition of calculating outcomes allows you then to correct if you are blown off course by reality, or at least to generate fresh rules for next time. But the North-West Passage? There be dragons. It may not even exist. All you can do is get the best boat, the best crew, and as many tools and resources as you can safely carry, for any eventuality that might arise. You will also take to frequenting taverns listening to tall tales from old sea dogs in case there is any wisdom in them, and collecting fragments of faded maps that might perhaps contain a vital clue at just the right time. So the emphasis is on readiness, and on maximizing your potential to greet evenly whatever you might encounter on the way.

Developing a truly rounded character that is ready for anything is a hard discipline, because it requires a commitment to the development of a whole range of virtues. Many of them may or may not see frequent use, but they all need to be supple. There is a famously devastating example of the importance of this. In the 1960s, the psychologist Stanley Milgram wanted to understand why, in the context of the Holocaust, so many people had behaved so very badly. The Milgram experiments involved a set of volunteers teaching word pairs to actors in an adjacent room whom they thought were fellow volunteers. If the 'pupil' got an answer wrong, the 'teacher' had to administer an electric shock, with the voltage increasing in 15-volt increments for each wrong answer. The actors were issued with tape-recorded reactions of screams and pleading, and encouraged to bang on the wall and protest as the shocks increased, then to fall silent. In some versions of the experiment, the teacher was pre-warned that the pupil suffered from a heart condition. While many of the teachers did respond to these protests, and questioned the purpose of the experiment, most continued after being told firmly by the experimenter that they must go on, and that they would not be held responsible for their actions. The experiment was halted only if the teacher continued to question the experimenter after being told to continue four times, or when they had administered the maximum 450-volt shock three times in succession. In a poll conducted beforehand, Milgram established a general prediction that an average of just over 1 per cent of the 'teachers' would progress the experiments beyond a very strong shock. In fact, Milgram found that 65 per cent of the teachers administered the experiment's final massive 450-volt shock, even though many of them were clearly very uncomfortable about doing so, and every single one of them questioned the experiment at some point.

One reading of the Milgram experiments is that they showcase our capacity for cruelty. But the American philosopher Robert Solomon argues instead that the experiments show in practice how hard it is to prioritize warring virtues, particularly if one is more 'supple' than the other. He sees it not as a lack of character in the 'teachers', but actually a conflict of character traits. In the Milgram experiments, the war was between obedience to authority, and human compassion. In the average human life, there are many more opportunities to practise obedience to authority than there are to practise compassion, making this virtue comparatively flabby (Solomon 2003). And current thinking in neurobiology about the 'plasticity' of the brain would support the idea that a given virtue needs to be actively practised in order for it to stick. If a virtue is not practised, our neural map for the virtue lapses, so the development of moral character can now be seen as the acquisition of a skill just like any other. This argues for the deliberate development of the less exercised virtues through practice. For example, one could deliberately practise moderation and thrift by diligently mending, reusing and recycling existing items, or by seeking to replace them with second-hand or budget substitutes rather than impulse-buying expensively at speed (see the Resources section for a character workout).

The snag about developing character is that almost by definition it takes time. The literature on habits is therefore helpful, particularly because in this context both developing virtue and weaning yourself off consumerism is extremely hard to do. It is hard not just because our psychology and our physiology will fight us; it is doubly hard because it is about our very self-concept and identity.

Habits are vital for our day-to-day operating. The neural shortcuts they represent save us valuable processing time so that we can get on with our lives. A bit like the army's Standard Operating Procedures, they code the mundane into our neuro-biological autopilot so that we can free up valuable cognitive space for novelty. And as we deploy these heuristics, our mental maps are reinforced, and the habits get stronger and even more effortless as time goes on. This also makes them extremely hard to shift.

In Charles Duhigg's book *The Power of Habit*, he tells the famous story of Febreze, an odourless air freshener developed by Proctor and Gamble in 1996. It was so brilliant that NASA used it to clean their shuttles when they returned from space. But it flopped as a consumer product. When the team looked carefully enough, they discovered that people were not using it because they had got desensitized to the bad smells around them, like tobacco or cats, there was no 'cue' to trigger usage. Further, if they did use it, there was no positive 'reward' – the bad smell simply disappeared. But when they viewed hours of video of people cleaning their houses, they noticed that at the end of each room or chore, the cleaner had a ritual – a smile, or a pat of the bed, or a plumping of cushions, as they signed off from the activity. So they relaunched Febreze with a fragrance, so that its absence when it had faded away would act as a cue; and a commercial that showed a person cleaning a room then using Febreze for a celebratory and fragranced spritz when they were done. Cue? My room no longer smells of Febreze. Routine – get out the can. Reward – heavenly smell. This in a nutshell is Duhigg's thesis – habits need all three, so if you want to change a habit, you need to disrupt a step in this process (Duhigg 2012, pp. 37ff.).

Suppose you take sugar in your tea. This behaviour is so hard-wired you do it automatically. Cue – kettle boils. Routine – line up the mug, the teabag, the sugar and the spoon. Reward – the first sip tastes perfect. But what if you want to make your dentist happy, or lose an inch off your waistline? We know from Pavlov's famous experiments what will happen when you hear the kettle boil, you will respond automatically, absent-mindedly stirring in the sugar while you talk over your shoulder to someone. The first sip is so normal it is not until much later you remember you were supposed to have given up sugar. So the smart people physically move the sugar bowl, to upset the routine. While you are trying to locate it, you are more likely to remember that you put it away to avoid temptation, and refrain from sugaring your tea.

In the context of shopping, one example of habit would be your internet or smartphone shortcuts. One-click ordering is the easiest habit in the world. So, if you wanted to adjust that habit, you would need to make time to change your default settings. Then your future one-clicking would be to well-researched and well-chosen websites, not just to the obvious ones.

Habits are supposed to be good. They are helpful ways to satisfy a need in the most efficient way possible. So before unwanted habits can be changed, the underlying need they satisfy has to be identified. But how long does it take to shift a habit? In their 2010 research, Phillippa Lally and her team found that it ranges from 18 to 254 days, with the average time being 66 days (Lally et al. 2010, p. 1007). So at least two months, on average. Given that you will need extra processing power to cope with the neurological disruption you will be causing, you will need to be able to afford this extra energy over a sustained period of time. But do not wait until you 'feel' like it. As Oliver Burkeman points out, we do not need to feel motivated to do something: we just have to do it. So we should simply note our procrastinatory feelings, and get on with it anyhow (2013, p. 69).

We know we could try harder to build our defences against being blown off course by consumerism, but what scaffolding might we use? The final section of the book offers a practical routine for auditing your health as a consumer.

8

The Consumption Audit

Introduction

Our final furlong concerns the star of consumption: you. Made in God's image, how you choose to invest your time and your talents, and who with, is at least as important as how you choose to spend your money and how this affects the earth's natural resources. So this section will look at consumption through all of these lenses: you, your time, your talents, your money, your relationships with people, and your relationship with the planet.

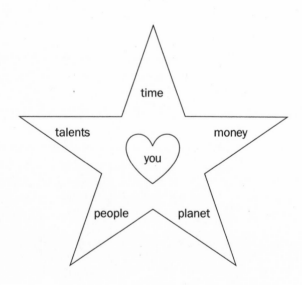

You

Wonderful, miraculous you. Mind, body and spirit. Do you cut corners around your health to save time? Perhaps you take your physical health for granted, by overeating or being too busy for exercise. God made you – you are special. Could you take care of yourself better?

Improved sleep is one crucial favour you could do yourself. Two recent books by Arianna Huffington and Vicki Culpin offer both an analysis of the problem and plenty of solutions. We now know that we need to sleep not only to repair our bodies, but also to form memories, so the less we sleep the more unreliable we become. The brain's executive function is replenished through sleep, so if your sleep is deficient, you start each day energetically behind. The executive function is how we self-regulate. Operating like the brain's PA, it organizes our behaviour, regulating and monitoring it in response to the environment, and it controls our actions and emotions. The executive function helps the brain to cope with complexity, creativity and problem-solving, and controls inhibition and the ability to assess risk. When we use willpower, energy is used up, as reflected in increased heart rate variability and a reduction in blood glucose levels. These levels need to be topped up for us to continue to function well, and rest and sleep are the best ways to do so. If we are to resist the lure of our usual consumer habits and to have the mental energy to ignore the compelling messaging all around us, this capacity is vital. So Culpin has this advice for poor sleepers. Try to avoid alcohol, caffeine and fatty, spicy or sugary foods two to three hours before bedtime. Exercise regularly, but not directly before you go to sleep. Keep your bedroom well ventilated, temperate, dark and quiet. Avoid naps after 5pm, and keep technology out of your bedroom. Reserve it for sleeping, and try a light snack like a banana or warm milk before turning in (Culpin 2018). Luckily for Christians, we have prayer, because the research shows that counting your blessings is the best way to prepare for a good night's rest (Huffington 2017). If you have a smartphone or wearable tech, you could try a sleep app. What do you notice? How could you improve your sleep? What might you do differently tonight?

You might be taking your mental and emotional health for granted too, not investing in nurturing the things that support it, like the relationships you rely on, and to which we will return. In his book on happiness, Richard Layard sets out the Big Seven factors affecting it: family relationships, financial situation, work, community and friends, health, personal freedom, and personal values (Layard 2005, p. 63). Are there any of these you might try to improve in your own life, or for those around you? And can you start keeping a track of your emotional highs and lows, to get a better sense of what triggers them? Perhaps that might help you make some different choices about what you take on or the company you keep; and remind you what you need to design into your life to restore peace and joy when times are tough.

And your spiritual life. We all take God for granted, which is a particular privilege of belief. But do we invest in our spiritual life through prayer and worship so that when our faith is tested we have the strength to prevail? As was mentioned earlier, one of the features of modern life in a consumer society is increased reports of decreased mental health. Some commentators call this acedia, or soul-sickness. Theos conducted a meta-study of research on religion and wellbeing, and found that the clearest correlation with all measures of wellbeing is 'social religious participation' which means active and regular participation in group worship or volunteering (Spencer *et al.* 2016). Could you do more of this? Meanwhile, an active prayer life will keep you focused on God.

Time

Time is money, they say. Some of us have time but not money. Some of us, quite the reverse. Few seem to feel they have this in balance, and of course it ebbs and flows over a lifetime. But it feels to me that we often use consuming to save time or to replace time. We save time through convenience shopping, and we replace time through guilt presents for absenteeism, or cash donations to causes we have no time to support. But time comes first. However, as you learn on day one on a time-management course, you can't manage time, only yourself. That is why it is so difficult.

On these time-management courses, an old favourite is to give everyone a metre of ribbon. First, you cut off the years you have already spent, and therefore how 'long' you still have left. Next, you cut off a third of it for sleeping. Next, you cut off lengths for time 'wasters' like commuting or illness. You keep going, with anything else that 'steals' your time, until all you have left is a very short piece of ribbon to show how much useful time you really have.

Of course we could use our downtime better, and we don't know the number of our days. But we are more sovereign over our consumption of time than we let ourselves believe. We may blame our lack of time on work or family, but we have chosen to consume our time in these ways, whether or not we now experience it as a tyranny. So the first step should really be to draw a pie chart about how you spend your time. Look back through a few weeks in your diary. Are you happy with the balance of your choices? How well does your use of time align with your values? Should you be gradually taking your time away from time-wasters into areas of your life where time will bless you? And even if you currently feel that 80 per cent of your time is proscribed, how could you restructure the balance of it so that you have captaincy again, and can invest your time in better ways?

Talents

Perhaps the central meaning of being created in God's image is that we are crafted to be creators too. I wonder if you know what your creative talents are? Often we sleepwalk into an occupation and perform it well enough to prosper, without really developing our real gifts and skills. Sometimes we are lucky enough to have tried something at school – music or drama or arts or crafts – and so know we could develop our potential in one of these spheres in the margins of our working lives. And if you are blessed with one of these kinds of public talents, you may already be leading your life in accordance with your gifting. But many of us are more prosaically talented, and sometimes that is a harder talent to locate. Here are some avenues to explore to help you find out.

First, what do you do that you do naturally, and that releases energy rather than absorbs it? While talent also involves graft in its implementation, when the task or the occasion is contemplated it often involves an initial lift in energy and a sense of recognition or joy, which can be a key indicator that you are on the right track.

Second, what would even your worst enemy admit you are good at? This is a helpful question because it shows you where people cannot do without your talent, even if they would normally try to avoid asking you for help. Who still comes to you anyway? Are there things you are sought out to do, even by people who would not normally ask you for a favour?

Third, do not be distracted by what people pay you to do, or by generic feedback on competence. You will recognize your talent because of how it makes *you* feel, not because of its effect on others. The educationalist Kurt Hahn sought to help every child at his schools to locate their 'grand passion'. One boy was apparently all at sea until it was discovered that he was extremely excellent at building walls. Whether or not a career in wall-building is either attractive or lucrative, nurturing your God-given talents feeds your soul and gives you strength for living out the rest of your life.

Few of us manage to find an exact match between our talent and a lucrative career, but being able to be truly excellent at gardening or baking or crosswords or board-games means that we always have somewhere to go to express ourselves fully. So say yes to random activities and opportunities. Try some night-classes or weekend courses. Ask people what they see in you. And when you find that gift, rejoice! Feed it, nurture it, find ways to use it – whether paid or unpaid. It is your birthright.

There have been generations of stoics doing soul-destroying jobs just to bring home the bacon. And perhaps the financial pressures on you mean that you have to make your talents a hobby rather than your main job. But regardless, build in time to husband your vital spark.

In tandem with this quest, might you also pay attention to how you do deploy your other skills through labour? Your work consumes you – your time, your energy, your attention and often your health. So perhaps you could be more selfish about this. Is the balance of risk and reward right, for the effort you are putting in? Does your labour contribute to global flourishing? Do you also give freely of your labour through volunteering when you can? There are certainly few people on their deathbeds struggling back into work to dial in for one final conference call. Do think about Brooks' eulogy virtues. What do you want them to be able to say about you at your funeral?

Money

There are several passages about money in the Bible, all of which ask pointed and difficult questions (see Resources), so Antonia Swinson suggests that we start any conversation about money by devising a form that signs all of our money and assets over to God (Swinson 2003). This is to remind us where it came from, and that we are just stewards of our wealth. So every penny that we spend is a spiritual decision. But what does it mean when you 'spend' your money? Is it spent? Of course not. It travels. The New Economics Foundation has devised a clever tool to track this, called the Local Multiplier 3 methodology. It varies a little by area, but to give you an example, their study in Northumberland found that every £1 spent with a local supplier was worth £1.76 to the local economy, and only 36p if it was spent in a national chain store. This is because of what they call 'blue hands'. If you imagine that everyone in your town has accidentally got blue paint on their hands, how much blue paint would be on your pound by the time it finished its journey? If you spend it in a national chain, the pound will probably head straight to London, or offshore, without getting any blue paint on it at all. If you spend it locally, the shopkeeper might take it out of the till to pop next door for a coffee; the waiter might take it next door to buy some milk; the checkout person might take it next door to the post office; the teller might give it to an OAP; the OAP might pop it in the church collection; the vicar might use it to pay the local plumber, who might use it to buy their lunch, and so on. That's a lot of blue paint. When they modelled it, they found that £1 spent locally was worth almost 400 per cent more. For the Council in Northumberland, this meant that if they were to spend just 10 per cent more of their annual procurement budget locally, it would mean £34 million extra circulating in the local economy each year (Sacks 2002). So think hard when you 'spend' your money. Your money doesn't leave the system, it stays within it. There is a great local initiative in Cape Cod. Their community campaign asks you to identify three local enterprises that you like having around and pledge to spend $50 a month with each of them. This is great nudge thinking. Browsing in that quirky bookshop then buying cheaper online just means that the quirky bookshop won't be there for much longer. So use it, or lose it.

In general, ethical spending tends to be the focus of responses to consumerism, and our spending behaviour certainly has an effect. As we have seen, markets are the meeting place for messages about supply and demand. In this way, your money acts like a vote. The more something gets voted for, the more it happens, which is why over time the market tends towards meeting the needs of the rich and powerful. Because the market is created by the sum total of all our individual actions and interactions that influence others in the market, we change it by changing these interactions. And Christians are already on the march. According to polling by the Evangelical Alliance, 59 per cent of Christians polled have chosen to move money to a more ethical form of investment; 68 per cent have chosen to do business with a cooperative or a mutual rather than a private company; 88 per cent have boycotted a particular company because of their practices; and 95 per cent have chosen to buy a product or service specifically because they knew it was produced fairly and ethically (Evangelical Alliance 2016). Indeed, the best example of where Christians have made a huge difference is the story of the fairtrade movement. Famously started in the UK in the 1970s by students from Durham, by 1998, the fairtrade market in the UK was worth around £17 million annually. Now it is now worth over £1 billion a year. In coffee alone, fairtrade now accounts for almost a quarter of the UK's roast and ground market. Fairtrade bananas were only introduced in 1996. Now a third of the bananas we buy are fairtrade, so in the UK we eat 3,000 fairtrade bananas every minute. We created an entirely new segment, just by choosing positively in the backs of churches and through catalogues, and now at the checkout. In their survey, the Evangelical Alliance found that 90 per cent of Christians buy fairtrade (Evangelical Alliance 2016).

As well as spending positively, spending can be withheld. Consumer boycotts have a noble history, from historical sugar and chocolate boycotts over the slave trade and indentured labour, to boycotts of Apartheid South Africa. Modern campaigns over plastics, animal testing, the fur trade, poor environmental and fishing practices, sweatshop labour, and human rights abuses, have resulted in several company climbdowns, in the face of falling sales and negative publicity, and social media has made it even easier for these campaigns to hit home.

More strategically, consumer action can change the dynamics of the marketplace quite specifically. In 2014, the Archbishop of Canterbury launched a task group on responsible savings and credit. Amid shocking stories about the predatory and exploitative practices of the payday lenders like Wonga, the Archbishop pledged to compete them out of business. The initiative saw the launch of the Churches Mutual Credit Union, in collaboration with the Church of Scotland, the Methodist Church of Great Britain, the Church in Wales and the Scottish Episcopal Church. It already has over 1,000 members, and assets of £3 million. More generally in the UK, over the last decade credit unions have doubled in membership and loans, and trebled in deposits

BUYING GOD

and assets. And since the cap on payday loans was introduced in 2015 – in part thanks to lobbying from the Church and the Lords Spiritual – the Citizens Advice Bureau reports an 86 per cent reduction in clients contacting them about payday loans, and that 38 per cent of payday loan market participants have left the market. These statistics suggest that the Archbishop's pledge is well on its way towards being achieved (Welby 2016).

One of the most formidable lobbies in the world is the US National Rifle Association, but they only have around 4 million members. In the 2011 Census there were over 36 million Christians in the UK. Here is an example of what could be achieved with scale. Just a modest one, by way of illustration. How many pairs of shoes do you own? Apparently, women own 20 pairs of shoes on average, but wear only five pairs regularly. With men, it is seven, with only a couple in regular use. Let us imagine that just one person in every church donated a pair of shoes to Oxfam. There are estimated to be 37,500 Christian churches in England. That is 37,500 pairs of shoes. Say they sell for an average of £2 a pair. That is £75,000. That is safe water for 75,000 people. It is over 10,700 mosquito nets, 300 farmyards or 50 classrooms. It would fix over 3,400 wells or educate 4,000 children. Just one person in each congregation, donating just one pair of unwanted shoes. Think what else we could do if we organized.

Bank Statements

Perhaps the best way to audit your individual spending is to develop an obsession with your monthly bank statement. Are you proud of it as a statement of your consumption?

First, are you proud of where you bank? Do you have more than one account, and could you spread your favours so that you are banking as ethically and productively as possible? Any savings you have could perhaps be invested in a credit union, or in peer-to-peer lending, or micro-finance schemes like Five Talents, and in the UK you can now do this tax-efficiently through an

118

ISA. Any social investment you make ensures that your resting money helps someone in need or invigorates social enterprise. It is now far easier to switch accounts, and there are initiatives like Move Your Money that score banks for you against ethical criteria. And if you don't save, perhaps you might start putting away just a little each month, just in case. Even £500 in the bank is sufficient in most cases to keep people away from payday lenders. Half of all payday loans are made for things like washing machines and cars breaking down, or temporary absences from work, or gaps in benefits payments. These are also the reasons why so many people have to use foodbanks. Any nest egg, however small, would help you avoid debt.

Next, your bills. Are your utilities as green as they should be, or are you still consuming fossil fuels? In recent years, Christian Aid, Tearfund and A Rocha have facilitated campaigns to help churches go green and switch their energy supply to renewables. One campaign, the Big Church Switch, saw over 700 churches switch to green energy. Online, sites like the Green Electricity Marketplace and the energy section on Ethical Consumer can help you find a better provider. Ethical Consumer also advises about phone providers and handsets.

Income. Does yours come from labour? If so, are you proud of your employer's consumption of you? Do you work well and hard, and are you paid fairly for your time and talent? Or perhaps your income derives from a pension or some investments. Are you actively managing these portfolios so that those running them for you are clear about your priorities? The ShareAction organization online can help you with this. Perhaps your income derives from benefit payments. Are you playing as fair as you can with the system, in spite of its flaws and the hardships you face?

Charitable giving. You may or may not tithe, but one suggestion is to start with the amount you feel you should donate, and work out your household budget from what you have left, rather than the other way around. Given that all you have is entrusted to you for stewardship by God, how are you using his wealth to serve his purposes? Can you give as a regular commitment – however small – to make your donations reliable and tax-efficient for the charities you support? Are you happy that your current giving is an accurate report of how you are expressing solidarity for those around you who are in need? The Macaskill book suggests some charities that are particularly effective in providing help. And you can double-count some of this effort by shopping in charity shops, shopping online through charity portals like Give as You Live, or signing up for credit cards – if you need them – that support charities every time you make a transaction. And if you have no money to donate, you may be able to offer charities your time, expertise and prayers, and any spare items you have that their shops might sell.

Cash. Please do use cash with local businesses to keep their banking costs down. But please don't collude with tradesmen to help them avoid paying tax. In a recent survey, the Evangelical Alliance found that only 39 per cent of Christians polled had never done this, so there is clearly room for improvement (Evangelical Alliance 2016).

Debt. Perhaps some of the entries on your bank statement are repayments for a mortgage or loan. How does this debt make you feel? If you are feeling consumed by it, what might you do to seek help?

Other spending. Do the proportions feel about right, in terms of expenditure on the various categories? Are you planting trees to offset unavoidable business travel? And are you spreading your spending to include businesses that need your support, even if they may cost a little more? Could you alter your pattern of spending next month to favour more ethical enterprises? Of course this process is fraught with dilemma. We may deplore Amazon and Ebay's tax gymnastics, but they offer a platform for thousands of small traders to operate, and they keep the Royal Mail afloat. And many demonized multinationals trailblaze environmentally and provide the country with much-needed employment and tax revenue. What constitutes an ethical business varies, but the more we can encourage these 'nice' games by choosing to spend with them, the faster we will convert the marketplace.

And is there anything that is not on your bank statement that should be there?

It is quite a salutary process, auditing your bank statement. But if we all did it, the economy would start inexorably to turn back towards God. It takes time to develop your ethical shopping databases. And you may need to be prepared to sacrifice the quick fix of a one-click order for a transaction that delivers more for the Kingdom. But if we don't do it, who will?

People

If you look at how you spend your time, the odds are that you are likely to notice that you spend less time on relationships than you had intended. We get so angry with multinationals 'free-riding' on societal goods, but we often take our own support networks for granted. This is a hidden example of selfish consumption – taking money out of a bank we don't always invest in. And it is not just about your nearest and dearest, your friends, relatives and godchildren, it is about work colleagues, your neighbours, the church, the local community, and your wider citizenship role. How healthy is the balance between your consumption of them and your investing in them?

More broadly, our faith teaches us that while money, time and the material world are finite, love is not. A friend of mine once confided that he had been secretly dreading the birth of his second child. He could not tell anyone, but he was desperately worried that he could not possibly love the second child as much as he totally and overwhelmingly loved the first, and did not want the second child to be short-changed. Of course, the baby arrived, and with the baby a fresh outpouring of total and overwhelming love. Love is the one string we have to our bow that is infinitely generative. But we often confuse it with time and money and our physical presence, and feel it is a rationed item. We consume God's love and the love of others, and we husband it greedily. But how could we love if our time was unlimited, our money was unlimited, and our capacity was unlimited? Perhaps this is the crowing measurement of our ethical consuming, if we could count all our transactions for love.

So find a piece of paper and map your relationships on it. You could also map your interactions with people day-to-day, both in person, online and on the phone. Next, code the lines between you for health – red, amber or green. Overlay against this your evaluation of how much you love each person. Where is this in balance, and how do you keep it there? Where is it out of balance, and how could you get it back in kilter? You would feel instantly richer in spirit if you were able to improve on any of these relationships.

Planet

We are people in relationship, not just with each other and in community, but with the world in which we live. Do you love the world enough? Like the idea that we 'spend' money, we have an idea that we can throw things 'away'. But where is away? Next time you groan about rinsing out a can for recycling, make it a prayer of thanks for the world God has made for us. What would it be like if you quietly and deliberately made being more green a faith priority?

One concept that repays attention is the notion of 'enoughness'. Modern capitalism presents unlimited choice as a supreme good, but the research would argue to the contrary. Not only does overproduction squander the planet's resources, but increasing choice suffers from the law of diminishing returns. Sheena Iyengar conducted a famous jam experiment as a simple illustration of how too much choice just paralyses consumers. In her experiment, she compared the behaviour of shoppers offered 24 jams to try with those offered just 6. Both were given coupons for a subsequent purchase, but those exposed to the larger selection seemed confused by the array of options, and tended to leave the shop empty-handed. A comparison across the groups showed that while 30 per cent of those customers offered the smaller selection bought jam, only 3 per cent of those offered the larger selection did so (Iyengar 2011, pp. 184–7). Too much choice can be tiring, and can trigger guilt and regret, because there are too many options to evaluate. Some people take decision fatigue to extremes, with Steve Jobs famously wearing the same outfit every day – black turtleneck, blue jeans and trainers – in order not to waste valuable mental energy first thing in the morning. This might not appeal, but are there areas of your life you could simplify by limiting choice for yourself and being more content with enough?

Another angle on reducing resource consumption concerns the weightless economy. In 2006, the Comino Foundation commissioned a report from the Cambridge econometricians CEBR to model the effect on the environment if there was a shift away from the consumption of manufactured goods towards increased consumption of services and 'experiences'. Their model showed that even a 10 per cent shift towards the weightless economy would reduce greenhouse gases by 6 per cent, because intellectual, aesthetic, spiritual, physical and social activities, rather than the purchase of material goods, consume fewer of the earth's natural resources. Specifically, their model suggested that the consumption of electricity would reduce by 5 per cent, coal by 11 per cent, and natural gas by 8 per cent; and that the UK's extraction of oil and gas would reduce by 17 per cent (CEBR 2006). Of course, this is just a model, but their findings agree with other research on patterns of consumption. So next time you buy a present for someone, could you gift them an experience instead?

My favourite writer on this subject is Ruth Valerio (see Bibliography). Her books are full of challenging questions about how we choose to live. One of the most challenging questions you could ask yourself when you are next shopping is: why am I buying this if I cannot recycle it? This particularly applies to single-use plastic, but also to clothing. For example, nylon takes over 30 years to biodegrade in landfill, which is why creative reuse or donation to a charity shop is a better alternative than the bin.

The other challenging question is about cost. Very few things are genuine bargains. If it is cheap, someone else is paying. This may be about poor labour standards, supply chain abuse, or resource exploitation. So asking yourself about the 'true' cost of whatever you are looking to buy – and researching online if possible – will help you to avoid any inadvertent support of irresponsible brands.

Audit

You might like to undertake the following audit of your consumption to see what you could do to improve your own prosperity. But before you do, Tim Jackson's is a lovely note to conclude on:

> At the end of the day, prosperity goes beyond material pleasures. It transcends material concerns. It resides in the quality of our lives and in the health and happiness of our families. It is present in the strength of our relationships and our trust in the community. It is evidenced by our satisfaction at work and our sense of shared meaning and purpose. It hangs on our potential to participate fully in the life of society. Prosperity consists in our ability to flourish as human beings – within the ecological limits of a finite planet. The challenge for our society is to create the conditions under which this is possible. It is the most urgent task of our times. (2013, pp. 66f.)

Consumption Audit (also replicated in the Resources section)

You

1 How could you improve the quality of your sleep?
2 What could you do to improve your diet?

3 How else might you improve your physical and mental health?

4 Which virtues could you plan to practise more in your life?

5 If you loved yourself as much as God loves you, what could you do to convince yourself of this great love?

Time

1 How might you gain more control over how you use your time?

2 What more could you do to align your use of time with your values?

3 If you had more time, how would you spend it?

4 How could you programme in these things anyway?

5 Where could you 'spend' some of your time more profitably?

Talents

1 What are your strengths? How do you know?

2 What activities give you energy?

3 What would even your worst enemy have to admit you're really good at?

4 Where in your life could you use your talents more?

5 What could you do next to develop your talents?

Money

1 What is your money supporting?

2 Looking at your bank statement, what changes could you make that would make you prouder of it next month?

3 What alternatives are possible for those transactions that make you uncomfortable?

4 How might you save enough for a rainy day?

5 What more could you give or lend, and where?

People

1 Which of your relationships need more work?
2 What more could you do to be a better friend and neighbour?
3 Who in your family needs more love from you?
4 Who in your neighbourhood needs more love from you?
5 Who in the world needs more love from you?

Planet

1 How much is enough for you?
2 What could you give away?
3 What do you throw away, and where does it go?
4 How could you optimize your energy use?
5 What could you do to love our planet more?

Conclusion

It is the future. I'm an old lady now. I live with some of my oldest friends. We first lived together in London after university. We've moved in together again, in an old Scottish castle, to live out our last days. Most of us still have our spouses, and our kids come regularly to visit with the grandchildren, who keep us young. We're part of a networked community who pool our resources and share our skills. Most of us had rich professional lives, so we now give back our skills through online mentoring and consultancy. Some of this is to people, and some to help improve the AI in our android colleagues. We also host visitors and events, and still run some bespoke seminars in our lovely library. In return, we have access to local tradesmen, support staff and carers to keep us and our home functioning well, and we are given fresh food from local producers. We keep our loch stocked with fish, and our land is used for farming by the local community. Our energy is a mix of ground-source heating and solar, and we host a wind farm on our land.

There is money, of course, but we seldom need to use it. It feels rather mediaeval going back to tally sticks, but the digital world makes that the easiest way to operate. The money we do have is invested through an amazing group of social investors. They target initiatives globally that use access to technology to drive development, particularly through education and access to health services. Our pensions are also ethically invested, and the new realtime shareholder toolkit means we can actively monitor and influence what companies are doing on our behalf. We invest some of our capital in the local credit union and in peer-lending platforms, so that all of our money is deliberately put to work.

I mustn't boast, but let me tell you about the grandchildren, because they make me so proud. Between them, they really showcase the way the world now works. It's been a weird transition, getting used to the reality of hybrid working with AI, and the citizen wage has been a real game-changer for how people feel about working.

Isabel loves shopping. She loves it so much that she does it for a living. Most of us are too busy to make good purchasing decisions, and she's an expert, both online and off. Modern barcoding has to tell you everything about anything you buy, so ethical screening is far easier. The international standards about supply chain, staff policies, governance and global citizenship give you a very quick RedAmberGreen, so you can be mindful of what your purchases really cost, in the widest sense. She gets commission on her purchases, and loads of freebies, which supplement her citizen wage, but she's doing what she loves so seems carefree.

Mark works for the Co-op. Not the Co-op I remember from the old high streets, but a huge global enterprise inspired by the growth of Mondragon in Spain. It is the most massive conglomerate and does everything. It seems that they can meet your every need, cradle to grave. He laughs when I tell him that Virgin used to try to be like that. I worry it's too big, but I think their membership structure helps keep governance possible by incentivizing the flow of information. Anyway – he's in charge of human–AI relations there. He has a background in both psychotherapy and cybertraining, so it's great he's found a role straddling this boundary.

Jo is a doctor. I find her role impossible to fathom. Most of what used to be done by doctors in my day is done by robots now. She describes herself as a health facilitator, helping people navigate their way through the labyrinth of self-help tools and devices, and bespoking wellbeing plans for them. I suppose it's a bit like coaching or cheerleading, and she needs to know enough medicine to spot when the machines get it wrong. I suppose it is a bit like pilots being able to land planes in an emergency. Don't tell her, but I still prefer going to the community nurses who just give it to you straight and you know they are on your side.

Tim works for the government. He's in the Department for International Co-operation, and his section is responsible for identifying UK intellectual property that should be shared internationally to fuel development elsewhere. Inventors don't pay to register their intellectual property any more, they are paid a fee to register, so that their know-how can be pooled for global benefit. I don't really understand how that works, but he says it's really financed by investors, because it accelerates the development of new businesses globally, and the market can predict what's downstream from the flow of registrations here. He used to work in the section responsible for sharing skills and know-how, although most of it is done by the bots these days.

Grace is a storyteller. At school she was very taken by the tale of Robert Burns collecting Scottish folk music by traveling around the country listening to people singing and playing. After school she travelled the world collecting stories, through interpreters and through drawings and through music and through dance. She's a contributor to a global archive that is seeking to preserve these stories for the future, as more and more people leave behind their oral traditions and their village settings to participate in the global market. She says that our stories tell us who we are, and why we matter, so we forget them at our peril. When she's not travelling to the four corners of the world collecting more, she goes into schools to hold the children spellbound with her stories. She tells us them, too, when we all gather together of an evening in front of the great fire, and it feels like such an ancient and right thing to do. We often say compline there too, when the chapel is too cold.

Thank you for indulging me, but they make us very proud! I wonder what on earth the world will be like for their grandchildren?

As William Gibson said, 'the future is already here—it's just not very evenly distributed'. I wonder what you recognized in that story? Of course all of it is already happening, somewhere in the world. But what would it take to make this kind of future more evenly distributed? Not much. Just a few of us, clustered together, behaving consistently well, until our actions become contagious. And the more of us that do it? The faster the wheel will turn.

I explained why earlier on in the book, using game theory. You can teach your children this by reading them *Mr Happy*, by Roger Hargreaves. In the story, Mr Happy meets Mr Miserable. He invites him to come and live with him in his house in Happyland. And ever so slowly, Mr Miserable's mouth stops turning down at the corners. Then it starts turning up at the corners. And eventually, Mr Miserable does something that he's never done in the whole of his life before. He smiles.

Or perhaps you prefer your Bible. In 2 Kings 5 is the story of Naaman, the commander of the armies of Syria. He has leprosy, and the king hears that there is a prophet in Israel who might be able to cure him. Laden with gold and silver, Naaman sets out, and arrives with his horses and chariots at the house of Elisha. But rather than coming out to greet the great man, Elisha sends him a messenger, telling him that if he goes and washes in the Jordan seven times, he will be cured. Naaman, expecting drama, is angry that that he is being fobbed off with something so prosaic. So he leaves. Eventually, he is persuaded to give the Jordan a go, and is cured. It really was that simple.

Consumerism is a desire that is susceptible to sin because it can be misdirected. And as a search for identity and completeness, it needs a theological narrative to release it from the infinite loop of insatiable selfishness. But it is a crucial part of our DNA that we should embrace not deny, if we can school it properly and direct it towards God. Christians should really find this easier than we seem to, because our faith has all the answers. Buying goods or buying gods? We know the Logos (λόγος) beats the logo. But if we really buy God – we wholeheartedly believe, and we consume in his name – we shall not fail.

Perhaps like Naaman we thought we could only redeem consumerism with a huge drama, involving massive legal and cultural change. But we could all be cured rather more easily. We just need to do something ordinary, but repeatedly, with intent. We simply need to hold fast to our liturgy, and preach the gospel. And we need to do so primarily through the fourth theology box, social liturgy (see p. 62), because we are in the public square, which means we need to risk genuine dialogue and do as much listening as we do talking.

Desire is a tricky word. It sounds dodgy. So perhaps we need to baptize the term, too, and re-describe the language game at play. It is not about desire, it is about yearning. Everyone we see who is storing up treasures on earth, building walls around themselves with stuff, they are not evil, just lost. And we can help them find their way home. But we will only have the authority to do so if we have first removed the plank from our own eye. And this requires from us a renewed pledge, to get out of our own way and allow grace to reign in our hearts:

And so the yearning strong, with which the soul will long,
   Shall far outpass the power of human telling;
For none can guess its grace, till he become the place
   Wherein the Holy Spirit makes His dwelling.

Resources

1   The Consumer's Prayer

God my creator,
All that I have is yours.
Send me out to be salt and light in your marketplace.
Guide my purchasing today so each transaction does your will.
Hallow my footsteps, and guide my every meeting.
Bless me, mind, body and spirit, so that I radiate your glory.
Bring closer to perfection all that is in me,
   so that I desire only you;
And lend me your grace and peace as I make life's choices.
Amen.

2 A Month of Virtue

This virtue workout invites you each day to carry a question with you as you go about your daily life. The virtues are in no particular order, so feel free to arrange them in a different way. The list is based on work carried out by Clive Wright, Richard Higginson, John McLean Fox, and the Christian Association of Business Executives, about virtues and the principles of business life. I have adjusted them to include some of the kinds of virtues that Robert Solomon would worry that we do not practise enough. You might like to write your day's practice virtue on a Post-it note and stick it to your computer, or perhaps write it on a card in your wallet.

Day	Virtue	Challenge
1	Service	Where could you be of service today?
2	Excellence	What could you be excellent at today?
3	Achievement	What might you strive for today?
4	Creativity	How might you be creative about your day?
5	Mercy	Who could you be merciful towards?
6	Fair-dealing	Where might you practise even-handedness?
7	Trust	Who could you trust more?

8	Stewardship	Where could you be taking better care?
9	Justice	Where does an injustice need your attention?
10	Diversity	How are you drawing on diversity today?
11	Work–life balance	How well is your lifestyle aligned with your values?
12	Role-modelling	Who is watching you, and how are you setting them a good example?
13	Moderation	What could you do less of?
14	Thrift	Where could you save money today?
15	Generosity	Who needs some of what you've got?
16	Gentleness	Who could you avoid harming today?
17	Joy	Where might you encounter joy today?
18	Commitment	Who needs you to show stronger support?
19	Care	Where is there an opportunity for extra care?
20	Forgiveness	Today, who could you forgive?
21	Humility	Whose help do you need to seek out?
22	Courage	What could you face up to today?
23	Honesty	When could you practise honesty today?
24	Resourcefulness	If there was a solution, what would it be?
25	Prudence	Where might you find wisdom?

26	Gratitude	Who should you thank?
27	Prayerfulness	When can you find the opportunity today to spend time with God?
28	Listening	Who needs you to stop talking and start listening?
29	Charity	Where might you bestow your love?
30	Hope	What are you looking forward to?
31	Faith	What can you leave up to God today?

3   Consumption Audit

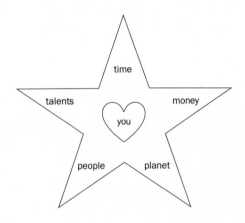

You

1 How could you improve the quality of your sleep?
2 What could you do to improve your diet?
3 How else might you improve your physical and mental health?
4 Which virtues could you plan to practise more in your life?
5 If you loved yourself as much as God loves you, what could you do to convince yourself of this great love?

Time

1 How might you gain more control over how you use your time?
2 What more could you do to align your use of time with your values?
3 If you had more time, how would you spend it?
4 How could you programme in these things anyway?
5 Where could you 'spend' some of your time more profitably?

Talents

1 What are your strengths? How do you know?
2 What activities give you energy?
3 What would even your worst enemy have to admit you're really good at?
4 Where in your life could you use your talents more?
5 What could you do next to develop your talents?

Money

1 What is your money supporting?
2 Looking at your bank statement, what changes could you make that would make you prouder of it next month?
3 What alternatives are possible for those transactions that make you uncomfortable?
4 How might you save enough for a rainy day?
5 What more could you give or lend, and where?

People

1 Which of your relationships need more work?
2 What more could you do to be a better friend and neighbour?
3 Who in your family needs more love from you?
4 Who in your neighbourhood needs more love from you?
5 Who in the world needs more love from you?

Planet

1 How much is enough for you?
2 What could you give away?
3 What do you throw away, and where does it go?
4 How could you optimize your energy use?
5 What could you do to love our planet more?

4 Useful Websites

Alternatives to Amazon

www.ethicalconsumer.org/boycotts/boycottamazon/amazon-shoppingalternatives.aspx

Books online

www.hive.co.uk/

Switch your bank account

https://medium.com/move-your-money

Switch your energy provider

www.greenelectricity.org/

Eco church

https://ecochurch.arocha.org.uk/

Instruct your pension fund manager

http://action.shareaction.org/page/content/greentlightlanding/

Join a credit union

www.findyourcreditunion.co.uk/home

Peer lending

www.zopa.com/

Social investment

www.triodos.co.uk/en/personal/ethical-investments/socially-responsible-investments/

Download an app to check who made your garments

www.notmystyle.org

General advice

www.ethicalconsumer.org

5 The Bible on Money

The Bible is not short of material about money. Of course, it is easy to argue that the marketplace was a lot less complex in those days, when poverty was mostly about lacking land and the means of subsistence, not being without coins. You would still search hard for a lost one, though. But the material is still very real, and very challenging. The following is not exhaustive, but is a collection of some of the most pertinent texts on this topic.

Parable of the Talents (Matthew 25.14–30)

Possibly the most referenced passage by business people is the Parable of the Talents, probably because it seems to recommend trading and even investment for profit, which is unusual given the standard line on usury. One of the things this passage makes me think about is the play on words: what talents has God given you, and how are you investing in their development? But reading the passage more literally, there seems to be positive endorsement about taking risk and rewarding enterprise, and negative treatment of too narrow an interpretation of what 'entrusting means' – the servant who buried his talent is punished, even though he was only doing exactly what he was asked to do in safeguarding it. And in this we perhaps see echoes of Jesus' frustration with those who would follow the letter and not the spirit of the law. The modern corporate addiction to shareholder value might be an example of this.

God and Mammon (Matthew 6.19–24)

This passage challenges those whose master is money. The hard saying that you cannot serve both God and money is for me interpreted by the line: 'for where your treasure is, there will your heart be also'. It is not so much that no one should work in the City, but that, if you do, you need to be crystal clear about your primary allegiance to God, because wealth carries the signal temptation that it can make you think that you do not need God. This is a hard passage to swallow, because modern culture is so brilliantly designed to wean us off God and on to the reassuring tangibility of material gain, backed up by a prevailing narrative that is about the need for facts not faith. And the tarnishing effect of money seems to be borne out by studies showing that richer people are generally more selfish than their poorer counterparts, probably because they no longer need to rely on social relationships so try less hard to sustain them.

The Unjust Steward (Luke 16.1–13)

Luke's version of the 'God and Mammon' passage, this one seems to encourage some very sharp practice indeed, but note that while the unjust steward is congratulated by his boss, he does not get his job back. One way to read this passage is to think about using mammon and the marketplace as a tool to build your ladder towards God, thus making them God's servant and not the other way around. The message still seems to be a confusing one, but perhaps while the master appreciates the shrewdness of his steward, the key message is still that the way you manage money and behave in the marketplace tells God all he needs to know about your true character.

The Rich Young Man (Matthew 19.16–26)

This passage has often been a difficult one for Christians with money, as it suggests that the true disciple would give it all away.

Modern interpretations have glossed it into being about the will-
ingness to give it up, which would indicate the sort of detachment
from it that indicates a healthy soul (see 1 Timothy 6.10 – 'For
the love of money is the root of all kinds of evil and in their
eagerness to be rich some have wandered away from the faith and
pierced themselves with many pains').

The Labourers in the Vineyard (Matthew 20.1–16)

This rather puzzling passage seems to approve exactly the sorts of
inequity that make office secretaries hate temps, full-timers resent
contractors, and unions go out on strike to get equal pay for
equal work. I think it is a very hard passage, and it is a bit like the
Prodigal Son in its central message. In business as in life, comparing yourself to others is not the best route to happiness. There will
be all sorts of reasons why there is inequality in the world, and
often you will not get what you feel you deserve. Indeed, if you get
what was agreed, you can't really complain. What is hard is that
a simplistic reading of this passage in isolation would in my view
encourage too much acceptance of injustice. The trick is to figure
out on whose behalf you are fighting. If it is in solidarity with the
weak, even though you too will benefit, your cause is just. If your
motivation is self-justification, with the benefit for others being a
rather secondary concern, your priorities are wrong.

While it is not about money, the passage for me that unlocks
all of these is this one from Genesis:

Jacob was left alone; and a man wrestled with him until day-
break. When the man saw that he did not prevail against
Jacob, he struck him on the hip socket; and Jacob's hip was
put out of joint as he wrestled with him. Then he said, 'Let
me go, for the day is breaking.' But Jacob said, 'I will not let
you go, unless you bless me.' So he said to him, 'What is your
name?' And he said, 'Jacob.' Then the man said, 'You shall no
longer be called Jacob, but Israel, for you have striven with
God and with humans, and have prevailed.' Then Jacob asked

him, 'Please tell me your name.' But he said, 'Why is it that you ask my name?' And there he blessed him. So Jacob called the place Peniel, saying, 'For I have seen God face to face, and yet my life is preserved.' (Genesis 32.24–30)

There are no easy answers in the Bible, particularly not on money. But we need every day to wrestle with what money means to us. We need to keep wrestling with it until it blesses us, even if it puts us out of joint in the process.

6　Six-Week Reflection Course

Week 1 – You

Reading

Psalm 91

1 You who live in the shelter of the Most High,
who abide in the shadow of the Almighty,
2 will say to the LORD, 'My refuge and my fortress; my God, in whom I trust.'
3 For he will deliver you from the snare of the fowler and from the deadly pestilence;
4 he will cover you with his pinions, and under his wings you will find refuge; his faithfulness is a shield and buckler.
5 You will not fear the terror of the night,
or the arrow that flies by day,
6 or the pestilence that stalks in darkness,
or the destruction that wastes at noonday.

7 A thousand may fall at your side,
ten thousand at your right hand,
but it will not come near you.
8 You will only look with your eyes
and see the punishment of the wicked.
9 Because you have made the LORD your refuge,
the Most High your dwelling place,
10 no evil shall befall you,
no scourge come near your tent.
11 For he will command his angels concerning you
to guard you in all your ways.
12 On their hands they will bear you up,
so that you will not dash your foot against a stone.

13 You will tread on the lion
and the adder,
the young lion and the serpent
you will trample under foot.
14 Those who love me, I will
deliver;
I will protect those who know
my name.

15 When they call to me,
I will answer them;
I will be with them in trouble,
I will rescue them and honour
them.
16 With long life I will satisfy
them,
and show them my salvation.

Discussion

God really loves you, in spite of all those things you feel worried about and ashamed of. And God has great plans for precious you. This passage reminds us to trust God's great love and to find renewal in him. When are the times that you have found this to be true? When have you struggled to see God in your life? What helps?

Activity

Mind, Body, Spirit. Draw a circle and divide it into these three areas. What are you doing to nurture yourself in each of these areas? What more could you do to show yourself more of God's love for you?

Week 2 – Time

Reading

Ecclesiastes 3.1–8
1 For everything there is a season, and a time for every matter
under heaven:
2 a time to be born, and a time to die;
a time to plant, and a time to pluck up what is planted;
3 a time to kill, and a time to heal;
a time to break down, and a time to build up;
4 a time to weep, and a time to laugh;
a time to mourn, and a time to dance;
5 a time to throw away stones, and a time to gather stones
   together;
a time to embrace, and a time to refrain from embracing;
6 a time to seek, and a time to lose;
a time to keep, and a time to throw away;
7 a time to tear, and a time to sew;
a time to keep silence, and a time to speak;
8 a time to love, and a time to hate;
a time for war, and a time for peace.

Discussion

What do you think about this passage? What does it say to you
about time? Why do you think we have time, and what for?

Activity

Thinking about last week, write down all the things that took up
your time. Looking at them, how do you feel about the balance?
What might you do to use your time well?

Week 3 – Talent

Reading

Matthew 25.14–30

14 'For it is as if a man, going on a journey, summoned his slaves and entrusted his property to them; 15 to one he gave five talents, to another two, to another one, to each according to his ability. Then he went away. 16 The one who had received the five talents went off at once and traded with them, and made five more talents. 17 In the same way, the one who had the two talents made two more talents. 18 But the one who had received the one talent went off and dug a hole in the ground and hid his master's money. 19 After a long time the master of those slaves came and settled accounts with them. 20 Then the one who had received the five talents came forward, bringing five more talents, saying, "Master, you handed over to me five talents; see, I have made five more talents." 21 His master said to him, "Well done, good and trustworthy slave; you have been trustworthy in a few things, I will put you in charge of many things; enter into the joy of your master." 22 And the one with the two talents also came forward, saying, "Master, you handed over to me two talents; see, I have made two more talents." 23 His master said to him, "Well done, good and trustworthy slave; you have been trustworthy in a few things, I will put you in charge of many things; enter into the joy of your master." 24 Then the one who had received the one talent also came forward, saying, "Master, I knew that you were a harsh man, reaping where you did not sow, and gathering where you did not scatter seed; 25 so I was afraid, and I went and hid your talent in the ground. Here you have what is yours." 26 But his master replied, "You wicked and lazy slave! You knew, did you, that I reap where I did not sow, and gather where I did not scatter? 27 Then you ought to have invested my money with the bankers, and on my return I would have received what was my own with interest. 28 So take the talent from him, and give it to the one with the ten talents. 29 For to all those who have, more will be given, and they will have an abundance; but from those

who have nothing, even what they have will be taken away. 30 As for this worthless slave, throw him into the outer darkness, where there will be weeping and gnashing of teeth."'

Discussion

One reading of this parable is that it commends our investment of our gifts and skills. We should not hide our light under a bushel but set it on a hill. Thinking of people in your life and in your congregation, where have you seen talent being nurtured well to fruition? How has that happened?

Activity

In pairs, talk about the talents that you know you have. How are you currently using them? Could you invest in them more? Are there any talents you used to have that you could rediscover? Are there any talented people around you who could do with your encouragement? What might you do to help?

Week 4 – Money

Reading

Matthew 6.19–24

19 'Do not store up for yourselves treasures on earth, where moth and rust consume and where thieves break in and steal; 20 but store up for yourselves treasures in heaven, where neither moth nor rust consumes and where thieves do not break in and steal. 21 For where your treasure is, there your heart will be also. 22 The eye is the lamp of the body. So, if your eye is healthy, your whole body will be full of light; 23 but if your eye is unhealthy, your whole body will be full of darkness. If then the light in you is darkness, how great is the darkness! 24 No one can serve two masters; for a slave will either hate the one and love the other, or be devoted to the one and despise the other. You cannot serve God and wealth.'

Discussion

This 'God and Mammon' passage is so familiar there is a danger we stop hearing it, or we hear it rather too starkly and turn away in despair. The passage is really about our primary allegiance. Where have you seen the Church pay more heed to Mammon than God? And your church? And you?

Activity

Often we can serve both God and Mammon, but sometimes there is a conflict and we have to choose. Looking back over your life, where do you notice you have made these choices? What can you learn about what helps you choose well?

Week 5 – People

Reading

John 11.11–7, 17, 32–44

11 Now a certain man was ill, Lazarus of Bethany, the village of Mary and her sister Martha. 2 Mary was the one who anointed the Lord with perfume and wiped his feet with her hair; her brother Lazarus was ill. 3 So the sisters sent a message to Jesus, 'Lord, he whom you love is ill.' 4 But when Jesus heard it, he said, 'This illness does not lead to death; rather it is for God's glory, so that the Son of God may be glorified through it.' 5 Accordingly, though Jesus loved Martha and her sister and Lazarus, 6 after having heard that Lazarus was ill, he stayed two days longer in the place where he was. 7 Then after this he said to the disciples, 'Let us go to Judea again.' 17 When Jesus arrived, he found that Lazarus had already been in the tomb four days. 32 When Mary came where Jesus was and saw him, she knelt at his feet and said to him, 'Lord, if you had been here, my brother would not have died.' 33 When Jesus saw her weeping, and the Jews who came with her also weeping, he was greatly disturbed in spirit and deeply moved. 34 He said, 'Where have you laid him?' They said to him, 'Lord, come and see.' 35 Jesus began to weep. 36 So the Jews said, 'See how he loved him!' 37 But some of them said, 'Could not he who opened the eyes of the blind man have kept this man from dying?' 38 Then Jesus, again greatly disturbed, came to the tomb. It was a cave, and a stone was lying against it. 39 Jesus said, 'Take away the stone.' Martha, the sister of the dead man, said to him, 'Lord, already there is a stench because he has been dead four days.' 40 Jesus said to her, 'Did I not tell you that if you believed, you would see the glory of God?' 41 So they took away the stone. And Jesus looked upward and said, 'Father, I thank you for having heard me. 42 I knew that you always hear me, but I have said this for the sake of the crowd standing here,

so that they may believe that you sent me.' 43 When he had said this, he cried with a loud voice, 'Lazarus, come out!' 44 The dead man came out, his hands and feet bound with strips of cloth, and his face wrapped in a cloth. Jesus said to them, 'Unbind him, and let him go.'

Discussion

In this story, Jesus raises his friend Lazarus from the dead. He knew he was ill, but stayed where he was, until Lazarus had died. He knew he could bring him back to life and that it would be a sign. We cannot bring our friends back from the dead, but we can pay attention to them while they are still with us. And not just our friends, all the relationships we have in the world, and all those we rely on and who rely on us. Where do you see brokenness in relationship, in society, in community, in the churches? Is there anything your congregation could do to help?

Activity

Decide which of your relationships you could boost this week. What will you do?

Week 6 – Planet

Reading

Benedicite

29 Blessed are you, O Lord, God of our ancestors, and to be praised and highly exalted for ever;

30 And blessed is your glorious, holy name, and to be highly praised and highly exalted for ever.

31 Blessed are you in the temple of your holy glory, and to be extolled and highly glorified for ever.

32 Blessed are you who look into the depths from your throne on the cherubim, and to be praised and highly exalted for ever.

33 Blessed are you on the throne of your kingdom, and to be extolled and highly exalted for ever.

34 Blessed are you in the firmament of heaven, and to be sung and glorified for ever.

35 Bless the Lord, all you works of the Lord; sing praise to him and highly exalt him for ever.

36 Bless the Lord, you heavens; sing praise to him and highly exalt him for ever.

37 Bless the Lord, you angels of the Lord; sing praise to him and highly exalt him for ever.

38 Bless the Lord, all you waters above the heavens; sing praise to him and highly exalt him for ever.

39 Bless the Lord, all you powers of the Lord; sing praise to him and highly exalt him for ever.

40 Bless the Lord, sun and moon; sing praise to him and highly exalt him for ever.

41 Bless the Lord, stars of heaven; sing praise to him and highly exalt him for ever.

42 Bless the Lord, all rain and dew; sing praise to him and highly exalt him for ever.

43 Bless the Lord, all you winds; sing praise to him and highly exalt him for ever.

44 Bless the Lord, fire and heat; sing praise to him and highly exalt him for ever.

45 Bless the Lord, winter cold and summer heat; sing praise to him and highly exalt him for ever.

46 Bless the Lord, dews and falling snow; sing praise to him and highly exalt him for ever.
47 Bless the Lord, nights and days; sing praise to him and highly exalt him for ever.
48 Bless the Lord, light and darkness; sing praise to him and highly exalt him for ever.
49 Bless the Lord, ice and cold; sing praise to him and highly exalt him for ever.
50 Bless the Lord, frosts and snows; sing praise to him and highly exalt him for ever.
51 Bless the Lord, lightnings and clouds; sing praise to him and highly exalt him for ever.
52 Let the earth bless the Lord; let it sing praise to him and highly exalt him for ever.
53 Bless the Lord, mountains and hills; sing praise to him and highly exalt him for ever.
54 Bless the Lord, all that grows in the ground; sing praise to him and highly exalt him for ever.
55 Bless the Lord, seas and rivers; sing praise to him and highly exalt him for ever.
56 Bless the Lord, you springs; sing praise to him and highly exalt him for ever.
57 Bless the Lord, you whales and all that swim in the waters; sing praise to him and highly exalt him for ever.
58 Bless the Lord, all birds of the air; sing praise to him and highly exalt him for ever.
59 Bless the Lord, all wild animals and cattle; sing praise to him and highly exalt him for ever.
60 Bless the Lord, all people on earth; sing praise to him and highly exalt him for ever.
61 Bless the Lord, O Israel; sing praise to him and highly exalt him for ever.
62 Bless the Lord, you priests of the Lord; sing praise to him and highly exalt him for ever.
63 Bless the Lord, you servants of the Lord; sing praise to him and highly exalt him for ever.
64 Bless the Lord, spirits and souls of the righteous; sing praise to him and highly exalt him for ever.
65 Bless the Lord, you who are holy and humble in heart; sing praise to him and highly exalt him for ever.
67 Give thanks to the Lord, for he is good, for his mercy endures for ever.
68 All who worship the Lord, bless the God of gods, sing praise to him and give thanks to him, for his mercy endures for ever.

RESOURCES

Discussion

The Benedicite reminds us that the whole of God's creation praises him. But some of that creation is being prevented from doing so by human over-consumption. Imagine we could ask all of those listed in the Benedicite what they are saying to God. What would we learn?

Activity

What are you already doing to help the planet praise God? Where else could you adjust your lifestyle to honour the creation God has made? What changes will you make this week?

References and Further Reading

Michael Allingham, 2002, *Choice Theory*, Oxford, Oxford University Press.

Aristotle, *Nichomnmachean Ethics* at http://classics.mit.edu/Aristotle/nicomachaen.html.

Jamie Arndt, Sheldon Solomon, Tim Kasser and Kennon Sheldon, 2003, 'The Urge to Splurge: A terror management account of materialism and consumer behaviour', *Journal of Consumer Psychology* 14(3), pp. 198–212.

Jeff Astley, 2002, *Ordinary Theology*, Aldershot, Ashgate.

John Atherton, 1988, *Faith in the Nation*, London, SPCK.

John Atherton, 1992, *Christianity and the Market*, London, SPCK.

John Atherton, 1994, *Social Christianity*, London, SPCK.

John Atherton, 2000, *Public Theology for Changing Times*, London, SPCK.

John Atherton, 2003, *Marginalization*, London, SCM Press.

John Atherton, 2008, *Transfiguring Capitalism*, London, SCM Press.

Robert Axelrod, 1990, *The Evolution of Co-operation*, London, Penguin.

Adele Azar-Rucquoi, 2002, *Money as Sacrament*, Berkeley, Celestial Arts.

Tom Beaudoin, 2003, *Consuming Faith*, Lanham MD, Sheed and Ward.

Ernest Becker, 1973, *Denial of Death*, London, Sage.

Daniel M. Bell, Jr, 2001, *Liberation Theology After the End of History*, London, Routledge.

Daniel Bell, 1976, *The Cultural Contradictions of Capitalism*, London, Heinemann.

P. L. Berger, 1990, *The Sacred Canopy*, New York NY, Anchor Books.

K. C. Berridge and T. E. Robinson, 1998, 'What is the Role of Dopamine in Reward: Hedonic impact, reward learning, or incentive salience?' *Brain Research Reviews* 28, pp. 309–69.

Nigel Biggar and Donald Hay, 1994, 'The Bible, Christian Ethics and the Provision of Social Security', *Studies in Christian Ethics* 7.

Nigel Biggar, 2009, 'Saving the "Secular" – The Public Vocation of Moral Theology', *Journal of Religious Ethics* 37(1).

Dietrich Bonhoeffer, 1995, *Ethics*, New York NY, Touchstone.

Christopher Booker, 2004, *The Seven Basic Plots*, London, Continuum.

Luke Bretherton, 2008, 'Political Consumerism and Pursuing the Peace of Babylon: A case study in the politics of ordinary time', *Political Theology* 9(4).

Andrew Britton and Peter Sedgwick, 2003, *Economic Theory and Christian Belief*, Oxford, Peter Lang.

David Brooks, 2015, *The Road to Character*, London, Allen Lane.

Malcolm Brown and Peter Sedgwick (eds), 1998, *Putting Theology to Work*, London and Manchester, CCBI/WTF.

Malcolm Brown, 2004, *After the Market*, Oxford, Peter Lang.

Malcolm Brown and Paul Ballard, 2006, *The Church and Economic Life*, Werrington, Epworth Press.

Malcolm Brown (ed.), 2014, *Anglican Social Theology*, London, Archbishops Council.

Susan L. Buckley, 2000, *Teachings on Usury in Judaism, Christianity and Islam*, Lewiston NY, Edwin Mellen Press.

Oliver Burkeman, 2011, *HELP!*, Edinburgh, Canongate.

Oliver Burkeman, 2013, *The Antidote*, Edinburgh, Canongate.

Colin Campbell, 2005, *The Romantic Ethic and the Spirit of Modern Consumerism*, Great Britain, Alcuin Academics.

William T. Cavanaugh, 2008, *Being Consumed*, Grand Rapids MI, Eerdmans.

CEBR, 2006, *The Experience Economy: Global growth without disaster*, Cambridge, Centre for Economics and Business Research.

Jonathan Chaplin, 2008, *Talking God*, London, Theos.

John B. Cobb Jr, 1959, 'A Theological Typology', *The Journal of Religion* 39(3).

J. Severino Croatto, 1987, *Biblical Hermeneutics*, New York NY, Orbis Books.

Vicki Culpin, 2018, *The Business of Sleep*, London, Bloomsbury.

Edward T. Damer, 1980, *Attacking Faulty Reasoning*, Belmont CA, Wadsworth Publishing Company.

Hernando de Soto, 2001, *The Mystery of Capital*, London, Black Swan.

Doctrine Commission, 2003, *Being Human*, London, Church House Publishing.

Ulrich Duchrow, 1987, *Global Economy – A Confessional Issue for the Churches?*, Geneva, World Council of Churches Publications.

Charles Duhigg, 2012, *The Power of Habit*, London, Heinemann.

Avery R. Dulles, 2002, *Models of the Church*, New York NY, Doubleday.

Martin Edress, George Psathas and Hisashi Nasu (eds), 2005, *Explorations of the Life World*, Dordrecht, Springer.

David Erdal, 2008, *Local Heroes*, London, Viking.

Evangelical Alliance, 2016, Survey on Ethical Consuming via http://www.eauk.org/idea/mar-apr-2016-issuu.cfm.

J. N. Figgis, 1997, *Churches in the Modern State*, Bristol, Thoemmes Press.

Daniel Finn, 1996, *Just Trading*, Nashville TN, Abingdon Press/The Churches' Center for Theology and Public Policy.

David Ford, 2007, *Christian Wisdom*, Cambridge, Camberidge University Press.

Robert C. Ford and Woodrow D. Richardson, 1994, 'Ethical Decision Making: A review of the empirical literature', *Journal of Business Ethics* 13(3).

Duncan Forrester, 1989, *Beliefs, Values and Policies*, Oxford, Clarendon Press.

Hans W. Frei, 1992, *Types of Christian Theology*, New Haven CT, Yale University Press.

H. H. Gerth and C. Wright Mills (eds), 1970, *From Max Weber*, London, Routledge & Kegan Paul.

Philip Goodchild, 2007, *Theology of Money*, London, SCM Press.

Timothy Gorringe, 1994, *Capital and the Kingdom*, London, SPCK.

Timothy Gorringe, 1999, *Fair Shares*, London, Thames & Hudson.

Tobias Gössling, 2003, 'The Price of Morality: An analysis of personality, moral behaviour, and social rules in economic terms', *Journal of Business Ethics* 45.

Elaine Graham, Heather Walton and Frances Ward, 2005, *Theological Reflection: Methods*, London, SCM Press.

Gordon Graham, 1990, *The Idea of Christian Charity*, London, Collins.

Stephen Green, 2009, *Good Value*, London, Allen Lane.

Douglas Griffin, 2002, *The Emergence of Leadership*, London, Routledge.

M. Guest, K. Tusting and L. Woodhead (eds), 2004, *Congregational Studies in the UK*, Aldershot, Ashgate.

Luigi Guiso, Paola Sapienza and Luigi Zingales, 2002, 'People's Opium? Religion and Economic Attitudes', *NBER Working Paper Series*, #9237.

James M. Gustafson, 1988, 'An Analysis of Church and Society Social Ethical Writings', *The Ecumenical Review* 40(2).

Ian R. Harper and Samuel Gregg (eds), 2008, *Christian Theology and Market Economics*, Cheltenham, Edward Elgar.

Richard Harries, 1992, *Is There a Gospel for the Rich?*, London, Mowbray.

S. Hauerwas and W. H. Willimon, 1989, *Resident Aliens*, Nashville TN, Abingdon.

Noreena Hertz, 2003, *The Silent Takeover*, New York NY, Harper Business.

John Hick (ed.), 1977, *The Existence of God*, New York NY, Macmillan.

John Hick, 1985, *Evil and the God of Love*, Basingstoke, Macmillan.

Richard Higginson, 1993, *Called to Account*, Guildford, Eagle.

Richard Higginson, 2002, *Questions of Business Life*, Carlisle, Spring Harvest.

Richard Higginson, 2012, *Faith, Hope and the Global Economy*, London, InterVarsity Press.

Mike Higton, 2004a, *Difficult Gospel*, New York NY, Church Publishing.

Mike Higton, 2004b, *Christ, Providence and History*, London, T&T Clark.

M. Hilbert, 2012, 'How Much Information is there in the "Information Society"?', *Significance* 9(4), pp. 8–12.

Kenneth R. Himes, 2007, 'Consumerism and Christian Ethics', *Theological Studies* 68.

Dwight N. Hopkins, Lois Ann Lorentzen, Eduardo Mendieta and David Batstone, 2001, *Religions/Globalizations*, Durham and London, Duke.

Sue Howard and David Welbourn, 2004, *The Spirit at Work Phenomenon*, London, Azure.

Arianna Huffington, 2017, *The Sleep Revolution*, London, WH Allen.

John Hughes, 2007, *The End of Work*, Oxford, Blackwell.

Christopher Insole, 2004, 'Against Radical Orthodoxy', *Modern Theology* 20(2).

Lisa Isherwood and Dorothea McEwan, 1994, *Introducing Feminist Theology*, Sheffield, Sheffield Academic Press.

Sheena Iyengar, 2011, *The Art of Choosing*, London, Abacus.

Tim Jackson, 2013, 'Angst essen Seele auf – Escaping the "iron cage" of consumerism', *Wuppertal Spezial* 48.

Oliver James, 2008, *The Selfish Capitalist*, London, Vermillion.

Oliver James, 2007, *Affluenza*, London, Vermillion.

David Jenkins, 2004, *Market Whys and Human Wherefores*, London, Continuum.

Timothy Jenkins, 1999, *Religion in English Everyday Life*, New York NY, Berghahn Books.

David J. Jeremy, 1990, *Capitalists and Christians*, Oxford, Clarendon Press.

Paul W. Jones, 1989, *Theological Worlds*, Nashville TN, Abingdon Press.

Anthony Kasozi, 2008, 'The Role and Influence of Institutions in Economic Development in Uganda', PhD thesis, University of Hertfordshire.

David H. Kelsey, 1975, *The Uses of Scripture in Recent Theology*, London, SCM Press.

Betsy Kendall and Robert McHenry, 1997, *FIRO-B*, Palo Alto CA, CPP.

Anthony Kenny, 1998, *A Brief History of Western Philosophy*, Oxford, Blackwell.

Fergus Kerr, 1997, *Theology after Wittgenstein*, London, SPCK.

Jeremy Kidwell and Sean Doherty (eds), 2015, *Theology and Economics*, Basingstoke, Palgrave Macmillan.

Naomi Klein, 2001, *No Logo*, London, Flamingo.

Wesley A. Kort, 1992, *Bound to Differ*, University Park PA, Pennsylvania State University Press.

P. Lally, C. H. M. van Jaarsveld, H. W. W. Potts and J. Wardle, 2010, 'How are Habits Formed: Modelling habit formation in the real world', *European Journal of Social Psychology* 40(6), pp. 998–1009.

Odd Langholm, 1998, *The Legacy of Scholasticism in Economic Thought*, Cambridge, Cambridge University Press.

Richard Layard, 2005, *Happiness*, London, Penguin.

Stephen C. Levinson, 1983, *Pragmatics*, Cambridge, Cambridge University Press.

Michael Lewis, 2014, *Flashboys*, London, Allen Lane.

George A. Lindbeck, 1984, *The Nature of Doctrine*, Louisville KY, Westminster John Knox Press.

Jeanne M. Logsdon and Harry J. Van Buren III, 2009, 'Beyond the Proxy Vote: Dialogues between shareholder activists and corporations', *Journal of Business Ethics* 87.

Jeanne M. Logsdon and Harry J. Van Buren III, 2008, 'Justice and Large Corporations: What do activist shareholders want?', *Business & Society* 47(4).

Stephen D. Long, 2000, *Divine Economy*, London, Routledge.

William Macaskill, 2015, *Doing Good Better*, London, Guardian Books and Faber & Faber Ltd.

Alasdair MacIntyre, 2003, *After Virtue*, London, Duckworth.

George Marsden, 1999, 'Christianity and Cultures: Transforming Niebuhr's categories', *Insights: The Faculty Journal of Austin Seminary*.

Karl Marx, 1972, 'The Fetishism of Commodities', in David McLellan (ed.), 2000, *Karl Marx: Selected Writings*, Oxford, Oxford University Press, pp. 472–80.

A. H. Maslow, 1943, 'A Theory of Human Motivation', *Psychological Review* 50(4), pp. 370–96.

Charles Mathewes, 2012, 'Toward a Theology of Joy', prepared for the Yale Center for Faith and Culture consultation on Joy and Human Flourishing, via https://faith.yale.edu/sites/default/files/mathewes_toward_a_theology_of_joy.pdf.

Sean J. McGrath, 2014, 'The Theology of Consumerism', *Analecta Hermeneutica* 6.

M. T. McGuire and M. J. Raleigh, 1985, 'Serotonin-behavior Interactions in Vervet Monkeys', *Psychopharmacol Bulletin* 21(3), pp. 458–63.

Kenneth Medhurst and George Moyser, 1988, *Church and Politics in a Secular Age*, Oxford, Clarendon Press.

Jacques Melitz and Donald Winch (eds), 1978, *Religious Thought and Economic Society*, Durham NC, Duke University Press.

Mary Midgley, 1997, *Wickedness*, London, Routledge.

Mary Midgley, 1999, *Can't We Make Moral Judgments?*, New York NY, St Martin's Griffin.

Vincent Miller, 2005, *Consuming Religion*, New York NY, Continuum.

Stephanie Y. Mitchem, 2002, *Introducing Womanist Theology*, New York NY, Orbis Books.

Jerry Z. Muller, 2002, *The Mind and the Market*, New York NY, Anchor Books.

Barry J. Nalebuff and Adam M. Brandenburger, 1996, *Co-opetition*, London, HarperCollinsBusiness.

John F. Nash Jr, 1996, *Essays on Game Theory*, Cheltenham, Edward Elgar.

Robert H. Nelson, 1991, *Reaching for Heaven on Earth*, Lanham MD, Rowman & Littlefield Publishers Inc.

David Nicholls, 1974, *Three Varieties of Pluralism*, London, Macmillan.

H. Richard Niebuhr, 1956, *Christ and Culture*, New York NY, Harper Torchbooks.

Douglass C. North, 1990, *Institutions, Institutional Change and Economic Performance*, Cambridge, Cambridge University Press.

Michael Northcott, 2007, *An Angel Directs the Storm*, London, SCM Press.

Michael Northcott, 2007, *A Moral Climate*, London, Darton, Longman & Todd Ltd.

Michael Novak, 1991, *The Spirit of Democratic Capitalism*, London, Institute of Economic Affairs Health and Welfare Unit.

Michael Novak, 1993, *The Catholic Ethic and the Spirit of Capitalism*, New York NY, Free Press.

Oliver O'Donovan and Joan Lockwood, 2004, *Bonds of Imperfection*, Grand Rapids MI, Eerdmans.

Joan Lockwood O'Donovan, 2005, 'Then and Now: The schoolmen and fair trade', *Faith in Business Quarterly* 9(2).

Paul Ormerod, 1999, *Butterfly Economics*, London, Faber & Faber.

Paul Ormerod, 2005, *Why Most Things Fail*, London, Faber & Faber.

F. R. Palmer, 1973, *Grammar*, Harmondsworth, Pelican.

F. R. Palmer, 2001, *Mood and Modality*, Cambridge, Cambridge University Press.

Robert M. Pirsig, 1974, *Zen and the Art of Motorcycle Maintenance*, London, Vintage.

Raymond Plant, 2001, *Politics, Theology and History*, Cambridge, Cambridge University Press.

Karl Polanyi, 2001, *The Great Transformation*, Boston MA, Beacon Press.

Eve Poole, 2005, 'On the Use of Language in the Anti-Capitalist Debate', *European Journal of Business Ethics* 59(4).

Eve Poole, 2010, *The Church on Capitalism*, Basingstoke, Palgrave Macmillan.

Eve Poole, 2015a, *Capitalism's Toxic Assumptions*, London, Bloomsbury.

Eve Poole, 2015b, *God and Money*, Manchester, William Temple Foundation.

Eve Poole, 2016, *Ethical Consumerism*, Manchester, William Temple Foundation.

Eve Poole, 2017, *Leadersmithing*, London, Bloomsbury.

C. K. Prahalad, 2006, *The Fortune at the Bottom of the Pyramid*, Upper Saddle River NJ, Wharton School Publishing.

Ronald H. Preston, 1979, *Religion and the Persistence of Capitalism*, London, SCM Press.

Ronald H. Preston, 1983, *Church and Society in the Late Twentieth Century*, London, SCM Press.

Ronald H. Preston, 1987, *The Future of Christian Ethics*, London, SCM Press.

Ronald H. Preston, 1991, *Religion and the Ambiguities of Capitalism*, London, SCM Press.

Ronald H. Preston, 1994, *Confusions in Christian Social Ethics*, London, SCM Press.

Ben Quash, 2006, 'Following God: The ethical character of Christian life', Unit 3, Module H8, Southern Theological Education and Training Scheme, Salisbury.

Ben Quash, 2007, 'Size Matters – On the importance of a theological "middle distance"', working paper.

Richard H. Roberts, 2002, *Religion, Theology and the Human Sciences*, Cambridge, Cambridge University Press.

Leo R. Ryan, 1989, *Clinical Interpretation of the FIRO-B*, Palo Alto CA, Consulting Psychologists Press.

Jeffrey Sachs, 2008, *Common Wealth – Economics for a crowded planet*, London, Penguin.

Justin Sacks, 2002, *The Money Trail*, London, New Economics Foundation/The Countryside Agency.

Jonathan Sacks, 1997, *The Politics of Hope*, London, Jonathan Cape.

S. Savage and E. Boyd-MacMillan, 2007, *The Human Face of Church*, London, SCM Press.

Friedrich Schleiermacher, 1963, in H. R. Mackintosh and J. S. Stewart (eds), *The Christian Faith*, vol. 1, New York NY, Harper Torchbooks.

Friedrich Schleiermacher (trans. D. M. Baillie), 1922, *The Christian Faith in Outline*, Edinburgh, WF Henderson.

William Schweiker, 2004, 'Reconsidering Greed' in William Schweiker and Charles Mathewes (eds), *Having*, Grand Rapids MI, Eerdmans.

Peter Sedgwick, 1999, *The Market Economy and Christian Ethics*, Cambridge, Cambridge University Press.

Peter Selby, 1997, *Grace and Mortgage*, London, Darton, Longman & Todd.

F. Sergio, J. Blas, G. Blanco, A. Tanferna, L. López, J. A. Lemus and F. Hiraldo, 2011, 'Raptor Nest Decorations are a Reliable Threat against Conspecifics' *Science* vol. 331, Issue 6015, pp. 327–30.

Andrew Shanks, 1995, *Civil Society, Civil Religion*, Oxford, Blackwell.

David Sheppard, 1983, *Bias to the Poor*, London, Hodder & Stoughton.

Dirkie Smit, 1997, 'Bound to Differ? Wesley Kort on Theological Differences', *Scriptura* 63.

Adam Smith, 1997, *The Wealth of Nations*, London, Penguin.

Robert C. Solomon, 2003, 'Victims of Circumstances? A defense of virtue ethics in business' *Business Ethics Quarterly* 13(1), pp. 43–62.

Nick Spencer, 2016, *Doing Good: A future for Christianity in the 21st century*, London, Theos.

Nick Spencer, Gillian Madden, Clare Purtill and Joseph Ewing, 2016, *Religion and Well-being: Assessing the evidence*, London, Theos.

Glen H. Stassen, D. M. Yeager and John Howard Yoder, 1996, *Authentic Transformation*, Nashville TN, Abingdon Press.

Jeffrey Stout, 1990, *Ethics After Babel*, Cambridge, James Clarke.

R. S. Sugirtharajah, 2002, *Postcolonial Criticism and Biblical Interpretation*, Oxford, Oxford University Press.

Antonia Swinson, 2003, *Root of All Evil?*, Edinburgh, St Andrew Press.

Kathryn Tanner, 2005, *Economy of Grace*, Minneapolis MN, Fortress Press.

R. H. Tawney, 1948, *Religion and the Rise of Capitalism*, London, Pelican Books.

Shelley E. Taylor, Laura Cousino Klein, Brian P. Lewis, Tara L. Gruenewald, Regan A. R. Gurung and John A. Updegraff, 2000, 'Biobehavioral Responses to Stress in Females: Tend-and-befriend, not fight-or-flight', *Psychological Review* 107(3), pp. 411–29.

Robert H. Thouless, 1974, *Straight and Crooked Thinking*, London, Pan.

Stephen E. Toulmin, 2003, *The Uses of Argument*, Cambridge, Cambridge University Press.

David Tracy, 1981, *The Analogical Imagination*, London, SCM Press.

David Tracy and John B. Cobb Jr, 1983, *Talking about God*, New York NY, Seabury Press.

Ernst Troeltsch, trans. Wyon, 1960, *The Social Teaching of the Christian Churches*, vol. 2, New York NY, Harper Torchbooks.

Jean M. Twenge, 2017, 'Have Smartphones Destroyed a Generation?', *The Atlantic*, September, at https://www.theatlantic.com/magazine/archive/2017/09/has-the-smartphone-destroyed-a-generation/534198/.

Ruth Valerio, 2008, *L is for Lifestyle*, London, InterVarsity Press.

Ruth Valerio, 2016, *Just Living*, London, Hodder & Stoughton.

Andrew Walker and Luke Bretherton (eds), 2007, *Remembering Our Future*, Carlisle, Paternoster.

Max Weber, 2002, *The Protestant Ethic and the Spirit of Capitalism*, London, Routledge.

Justin Welby, 2016, *Dethroning Mammon*, London, Bloomsbury.

Samuel Wells, 2004, *Improvisation*, Grand Rapids MI, Brazos Press.

Wilf Wilde, 2006, *Crossing the River of Fire*, Peterborough, Epworth.

Rowan Williams, 2000a, *On Christian Theology*, Oxford, Blackwell.

Rowan Williams, 2000b, *Lost Icons*, Edinburgh, T&T Clark.

Rowan Williams, 2002, *Arius*, Grand Rapids MI, Eerdmans.

Walter Wink, 1992, *Engaging the Powers*, Minneapolis MN, Fortress Press.

Christopher J. H. Wright, 1983, *The Use of the Bible in Social Ethics*, Bramcote, Grove.

Clive Wright, 2004, *The Business of Virtue*, London, SPCK.

N. T. Wright, 1992, *The New Testament and the People of God*, Minneapolis MN, Fortress Press.

John Howard Yoder, 1992, *Nevertheless*, Scottdale PA, Herald Press.

Index

A Month of Virtue, 134–6
A Rocha, 119, 139
    see also ecochurch
Absolutist, see Theology
Academy, the, 34, 35, 37–8, 46, 57–9
acedia, 112
    see also Affluenza
achievement, 95, 134
    see also A Month of Virtue
addictive, addiction, xi, 59, 89, 97, 141
adverts, advertising, 70, 78–80, 83–4, 89, 91–2
agency theory, 71, 73–4, 76
    see also toxic assumptions
alienation, 21, 36
altruism, altruistic, xvi, xvii, 84, 86, 101–2, 104
Amazon, 120, 139
analogy, 34, 49, 102
    see also Tracy, David
Anglican, xiii, 4, 77
anthropology, anthropological, 20, 25–6, 28, 31, 48, 60
anxiety, 87, 99
apologetics, 38–9, 43, 59, 64
    see also Theology
Aquinas, Thomas, 12, 35
Areopagus, 97
Aristotle, 50, 53, 103–4
Arndt, Jamie, 99–100

Artificial Intelligence, 127–8
Ashridge Business School, ix, 105
asymmetric, asymmetrical, 57–9, 63
Athenians, 97
audience, xi, xii, 5, 34, 37–8, 52, 54–5, 57–8, 62–3, 65
    see also publics
audit, auditing, xi, 3, 109, 110, 118, 121, 124, 132, 137
Augustine, 14, 35, 87
Axelrod, Robert, xvi–vii

bank statement, 118, 120–1, 125, 138
banks, banking, 79, 93, 118–21, 125, 138, 139, 148
Barth, Karl, xii, 22, 47
bearded vulture, 80
Beaudoin, Tom, 91, 94
Becker, Ernest, 99–100
Beijing, 79
Benedicite, 153, 155
benevolence, 70, 104
Berger, Peter L, 87, 98
    see also Sacred Canopy
Bible, 97, 130f, 141–4, 145–55
Big Church Switch, 119
binoculars, 6
blue footed booby bird, 80
blue hands, 115
Bond, James Bond, 89

information, 62, 72, 75, 78–9, 90,
    103, 128
    see also game theory
innovation, 50, 65
insatiability, 83, 85, 88, 130
    see also desire
institutions, xiii, xiv, xv, 11,
    24, 74
intrinsic, motivation and values,
    xviii, 100, 103
introversion, 98
investments, investment, 71, 77,
    101, 116, 118–9, 127, 129,
    140–1, 148–9
Invisible Hand, the, 70, 72, 74–5
    see also toxic assumptions
Iyengar, Sheena, 122–3
    see also jam experiment

Jackson, Tim, 87, 124
Jacob, wrestling, 143–4
jam experiment, 122–3
James, Oliver, 87
jargon, 3–4, 40, 50
Jenkins, Timothy, 23
Jobs, Steve, 123
Jones, Paul W, 16, 20–5, 29–
    30, 58
    see also Theology
joy, 112, 114, 135, 148
    see also A Month of Virtue
justice, 22, 75, 135, 143
    see also A Month of Virtue

Kasozi, Anthony, xiv
    see also institutions
Kelsey, David H, 33
Kenny, Anthony, 53
kindness, 105
Klein, Naomi, 78, 92
    see also No Logo
Kort, Wesley A, 26–30, 58
    see also Theology

Krinks, Philip, x
Kübler-Ross, Elisabeth, xvii
    see also grief curve

laissez faire, 75–6
Lally, Phillippa, 108
landfill, throwing 'away', 122,
    123, 126, 138
language game, 7, 40–3, 131
    see also Wittgenstein, Ludwig
Layard, Richard, 112
    see also happiness
leadership, ix–x, xvii, 100
Lent group resources, 145
Liberation Theology, see Theology
limited liability, 71, 74–6
    see also toxic assumptions
Lindbeck, George, 40–3, 45–6, 48,
    50–2, 58
    see also Theology
listening, 64, 92, 105, 129, 131,
    136
    see also A Month of Virtue
liturgy, 4, 60–3, 102, 131
    see also Social Liturgy
Loades, Ann, x
Local Multiplier 3 Methodology,
    115
logo, 78–80, 92–4, 130
Lords, House of, 62, 77
love, 121–2, 124–6, 136–8, 143,
    146–7, 150–51
    see also A Month of Virtue

Macaskill, William, 101, 120
MacIntyre, Alasdair, 97, 102
Mammon, xi, 86, 142, 150
mandates, see Orders of Creation
marketplace, ix, 3, 70, 72, 75–6,
    84, 95, 117, 119–20, 133, 141–2
Marx, Karl, 50, 83, 97
Maslow, Abraham, 91, 98
materialism, 99-100